JOSH HAYDEN

REMISSIONING CHURCH

A FIELD GUIDE TO BRINGING A CONGREGATION BACK TO LIFE

ivp

An imprint of InterVarsity Press
Downers Grove, Illinois

InterVarsity Press
P.O. Box 1400 | Downers Grove, IL 60515-1426
ivpress.com | email@ivpress.com

InterVarsity Press® is the publishing division of InterVarsity Christian Fellowship/USA®. For more information, visit intervarsity.org.

All Scripture quotations, unless otherwise indicated, are taken from The Holy Bible, New International Version®, NIV®. Copyright © 1973, 1978, 1984, 2011 by Biblica, Inc.™ Used by permission of Zondervan. All rights reserved worldwide. www.zondervan.com. The "NIV" and "New International Version" are trademarks registered in the United States Patent and Trademark Office by Biblica, Inc.™

Scripture quotations marked MSG are taken from The Message, copyright © 1993, 2002, 2018 by Eugene H. Peterson. Used by permission of NavPress. All rights reserved. Represented by Tyndale House Publishers.

While any stories in this book are true, some names and identifying information may have been changed to protect the privacy of individuals.

"No Running in Halls" photo by the author.

"J. Hayden Benediction" original watercolor by Rev. Suzanne L. Vinson, artist and facilitator, whose work can be found at silvertreeart.com. Used with permission of the artist. Art & Lettering ©suzannelvinson. Text ©Joshua Hayden.

Excerpt of "A Rude Awakening" from *God Speaks Through Wombs* by Drew Jackson. Copyright ©2021 by Drew Edward Jackson. Used by permission of InterVarsity Press, P.O. Box 1400, Downers Grove, IL 60515, USA. www.ivpress.com.

The publisher cannot verify the accuracy or functionality of website URLs used in this book beyond the date of publication.

Cover design: Faceout Studio, Jeff Miller
Interior design: Daniel van Loon and Jeanna Wiggins
Images: Moment via Getty Images: © Neon, © oxygen; ©kathykonkle / DigitalVision Vectors via Getty Images; © Alice Adler / fStop via Getty Images

ISBN 978-1-5140-1055-6 (print) | ISBN 978-1-5140-1056-3 (digital)

Printed in the United States of America ⊗

Library of Congress Cataloging-in-Publication Data
A catalog record for this book is available from the Library of Congress.

32   31   30   29   28   27   26   25 | 13   12   11   10   9   8   7   6   5   4   3   2   1

"The demands of ministry are such that it can be easy for an established church's vision to be reduced to mere survival. In *Remissioning Church*, Joshua Hayden gives established churches a remarkable gift: an inspiring, practical, field-tested road map to rediscovering one's calling as a community on mission."

Tim Morey, lead pastor at Life Covenant Church in Torrance, California, and author of *Planting a Church Without Losing Your Soul*

"Here's the book that is needed by about 90 percent of all churches and 100 percent of all clergy in North America. Josh Hayden's book is an enthusiastic invitation to today's congregations to refit themselves for vital participation in Christ's mission. Practical, proven, biblical, and very wise, *Remissioning Church* is destined to help scores of churches find their way into the future."

Will Willimon, professor of the practice of Christian ministry at Duke Divinity School and author of *Changing My Mind: The Overlooked Virtue for Faithful Ministry*

"This book is a must-read for church leaders grappling with the challenges of guiding a congregation into a future both faithful to the gospel and meaningfully engaged with the needs and longings of their community. Hayden offers a thoughtful and practical vision for remissioning, and his humility and lived experience bring heart and credibility to every page. Hayden doesn't shy away from the difficulty of the journey but equips leaders with the tools and courage to embrace it. For those seeking to inspire and sustain meaningful change, this book is both a guide and a trusted companion."

Shannon Kiser, senior director of Fresh Expressions North America

"Not a few pastors of plateaued and declining churches have asked with Ezekiel of old, 'Can these bones live?' In *Remissioning Church*, Josh Hayden responds to this age-old question with fresh, insightful, and actionable answers. I encourage you to have the courage and the care to read, reflect on, and then act on this wise, winsome, and practical book that enables us to see and to say again and anew, 'Resurrection happens!'"

Todd D. Still, DeLancey Dean and Hinson Professor at the George W. Truett Seminary at Baylor University

"Many today struggle to accurately address church decline and the need for a fresh approach to the mission of the church. With a passion for pastors to step confidently into a new day for their church ministry, Dr. Josh Hayden draws from his own research and pastoral experience to demonstrate a transformational process of resetting the missional direction of the church for the immediate ministry context and beyond. Through careful consideration of the church's past and present journey, Dr. Hayden provides relevant and tested steps into a new vision for the pastor and the church."

Ken Pruitt, president of Leland Seminary

"Born out of Josh Hayden's doctoral study and decades of pastoring, *Remissioning Church* shows what a true field guide is: expertise and lived-out work. Josh's invitation is simple: Does the church matter to the community it resides in? The underlying sense woven throughout all of *Remissioning Church* is that Josh answers yes because he steadfastly loves the church."

Eun K. Strawser, pastor of Ma Ke Alo o and author of *Centering Discipleship*

"Most churches in the West, including church plants of the last couple of decades, are in desperate need today of rediscovering their purpose in radically changed contexts and taking the necessary steps to restructure their lives together for the sake of God's mission—the work of remissioning. I can think of no one better to guide us in that work than my friend and collaborator Josh Hayden. Here's a work of hope and courage, filled with great love for the church and God's kingdom and with grounded wisdom for the leadership needed for remissioning congregations."

Kyuboem Lee, Thomas Taylor Professor of Practical Theology at Missio Seminary and pastor in residence at Renewal Presbyterian Church in Philadelphia

"In *Remissioning Church*, Josh Hayden masterfully calls the church back to its essence—a humble, vibrant community empowered by the Spirit to embody God's transformative love. Through stories, wisdom, and prophetic challenge, this book invites leaders and congregations to confront fear, embrace vulnerability, and pursue authentic renewal. Avoiding quick fixes and shiny solutions, Hayden instead charts a path of intentional discipleship and courageous pruning. This book is a clarion call for churches to thrive in Christ's mission—a gift to anyone longing to see the church reawakened."

Lisa Rodriguez-Watson, national director of Missio Alliance

"I wonder where this book has been all my ministry? All my life? For decades evangelicals planted churches. Now the cool kids want to turn around failing churches. But it's so much harder. Josh Hayden has the scars to show he knows it. And 'revitalize'? I'll never use the word again. Hayden's 'remission'? More of this, please, Lord Jesus."

Jason Byassee, senior pastor of Timothy Eaton Memorial Church and trustee of Wycliffe College at the University of Toronto

TO FIRST BAPTIST CHURCH ASHLAND:

your faithfulness, courage, and love for your neighbor has

helped me understand the power of the mission of God.

Serving with each of you has been one of the

most humbling gifts in my life.

TO SHEY, ROWAN, AND ELI:

your gentle courage, faithful resilience,

and dedicated perseverance helps me to

see Jesus and love our neighbors.

TO REV. DR. WILLIAM THOMAS:

thanks for seeing me and helping to name my calling

before I had words. I look forward to seeing you again

in that place where there are no more tears or pain.

CONTENTS

———————————— PART ONE ————————————

THE JOURNEY OF A THOUSAND MILES STARTS SOMEWHERE | 1

1 The Gift of Remissioning   3

2 Remissioning Through Descent   14

3 Finding Ourselves in the Remissioning Story   21

4 Remissioners Shift from Ownership to Stewardship   28

———————————— PART TWO ————————————

PRACTICING RESURRECTION THROUGH CREATIVE DESTRUCTION | 41

5 Creative Destruction: Remissioning from Death to Life   43

6 Remissioning with Fresh Eyes   52

7 Pruning for Growth in the Remissioning Garden   63

8 The Nature of Change in the Remissioning Journey   69

———————————— PART THREE ————————————

TRADITIONED INNOVATION | 85

9 Remissioning Starts with the End   87

10 Remissioning and the Work of Remembering   96

11 Burying Preferences for the Sake of Mission   106

12 Everything Is Liturgical (So Remission on Purpose!)   115

———————————— PART FOUR ————————————

DEVELOPING DISCIPLESHIP PATHWAYS | 125

13 The Four Spaces of Belonging in a Remissioning Context   127

14 Creating Shared Experiments to Grow a Remissioning
   Imagination   136

15 Movemental Discipleship for Remissioning Churches   146

16 Race, Class, and the Kingdom of God Are Essential
   for Remissioning   159

——————— **PART FIVE** ———————

REMISSIONING LEADERSHIP | *175*

17 Habits + Vision = Remissioning   *177*

18 Embracing Conflict as Remissioning Leaders   *185*

19 An Open Invitation for Remissioning Leaders   *194*

20 A Remissioning Path Requires New Metrics   *202*

21 Four Pathways for Remissioning   *208*

22 Dying to Live   *218*

Acknowledgments   *223*

Notes   *227*

PART ONE

THE JOURNEY OF A THOUSAND MILES STARTS SOMEWHERE

Translation is the church's birthmark as well as its missionary benchmark: the church would be unrecognizable or unsustainable without it.

LAMIN SANNEH, *WHOSE RELIGION IS CHRISTIANITY?*

BENEATHA: *Love him? There is nothing left to love.*
MAMA: *There is always something left to love. And if you ain't learned that, you ain't learned nothing.* (Looking at her) *Have you cried for that boy today? I don't mean for yourself and for the family 'cause we lost the money. I mean for him: what he been through and what it done to him. Child, when do you think is the time to love somebody the most? When they done good and made things easy for everybody? Well then, you ain't through learning—because that ain't the time at all. It's when he's at his lowest and can't believe in hisself 'cause the world done whipped him so! When you starts measuring somebody, measure him right, child, measure him right. Make sure you done taken into account what hills and valleys he come through before he got to wherever he is.*

LORRAINE HANSBERRY, *A RAISIN IN THE SUN*

Our eyes were opened, but too late.

ELIE WIESEL, *NIGHT*

1

THE GIFT OF REMISSIONING

Practice resurrection.

Wendell Berry, *The Mad Farmer Poems*

It's about following and imitating Jesus and *helping others follow
and imitate Jesus. It's meant for everyone and not just some.*

Eun Strawser, *Centering Discipleship*

A few months into my new adventure as a senior pastor in a
very established (150-plus-year-old) congregation, two experiences helped
me realize I might have misjudged the depth of change necessary in my new
calling. One Sunday in the greeting line after worship, a woman grabbed me
by the shoulders (without shaking my hand), pushed down, and said, "Young
man, this is how you stay put. We placed that pulpit on the stage for you to
stand behind, so quit moving around."

A few weeks later I did my first baptism and coached the congregation on
how to celebrate with the kids and adults who were committing to be disciples of Jesus and walk from death to life. I encouraged them to clap, cheer,
say "amen," and celebrate the moment with each person getting baptized
that day. In the greeting line after the service, a gentleman shook my hand
and said, "That was nice to celebrate baptism with so many people today and
to cheer them on. It's not how we do it here, but it was nice for today."

I had no idea that wandering a few steps from the pulpit while addressing the small crowd spread through a large sanctuary would cause so much discomfort. And who knew that encouraging some cheer during baptisms could be such a bother?

As I've worked with churches in different cultural, denominational, and geographic contexts, one thing has been abundantly clear: people resist change. Some resistance begins on the surface. For example, one church grew concerned when someone threatened to cut their twenty-one-step process for making punch at receptions down to a simpler process. Other means of resistance are more complicated. Some immigrant churches try to hold on to their native culture even as younger generations assimilate into the majority culture of their new home nation, leading to differing opinions on which language to use for worship.

The most common theme I've seen in dying churches is an overemphasis on shiny tools and technology that mask the decline of the congregation. One church near my home bought a large, overwhelmingly bright, impossible-to-read electronic sign for a building that can't hold more than forty people. They spent thousands of dollars on a sign for a back-country road where no one drives if they don't already know the church exists. This isn't much different from the thousands of churches that began broadcasting worship services online during the pandemic but never shared access to anyone outside the existing congregation. These churches put their hope in quick fixes and updated technologies, yet they still struggle or fail. They don't need revitalization. They need remissioning.

In 2019 a noticeable shift occurred in Protestant Christianity in the United States: more churches closed than opened (three thousand new churches formed and forty-five hundred churches closed for a loss of fifteen hundred).[1] While most church-planting networks have doubled down on starting new communities, is it possible to mature an established congregation out of its dysfunction and into health from the inside out? Is there something to be done about the large number of church closures besides abandoning them to start something new?

The starting point in the remissioning journey is a commitment to a central idea: people can change. And the idea that people, churches, institutions, and organizations *can't* change is antithetical to the good news of Jesus.

Don't get me wrong. People don't change easily. Churches, businesses, nonprofits, and other organizations don't evolve without struggle. People don't often want to change. But it's simply not true that people don't change.

This book is a story about hope and an invitation for church leaders and congregations to discover a pathway from death to life. We will explore stories about churches that are transforming into faith communities that are good for their neighborhoods and share tools that help remissioning churches pursue flourishing.

In a polarized, postmodern, and rapidly changing world, it's an uphill battle for established churches to defy their neighbors' skepticism that they're interested in the community's flourishing. And it's tempting to hide behind that struggle and avoid inviting real-life people into repentance and new life. But the alternative is death. A kind of dying that ends in the tomb and has no bearing on a shared future with God.

If I could pull the curtain back for a moment on this entire remissioning project and show you the wizard at the end of the yellow brick road, my hope would be this: you and your church would commit to making disciples who imitate Jesus and break the generational pattern of waiting until dropout, decline, or death to pursue a clear mission again.

Turn Up the Temperature

Established churches are on a journey. And to face the changes that happen on that journey, they embrace a common mantra: "The pain of staying must become greater than the pain of going."

That's because established churches need heat.

Have you ever heard of pyrophytic plants? That's right, fire plants (cue your favorite Super Mario fire flower memory!). Some trees and plants not only tolerate fire, but they also depend on its heat to further their species.

Some trees have fire-activated serotinous cones. For example, the long, skinny, sturdy lodgepole pines used to make tepees and cabins in the West produce cones that are sealed up with resin. For the seeds to be released, the cones need fire. During a forest fire, flames melt the resin, allowing the seeds to fall out and be scattered by the wind, gravity, and weather to germinate elsewhere.

Fire destroys many plants, organisms, and animals in its path. However, certain kinds of eucalyptus trees have special buds beneath the surface of their trunks that won't emerge until the bark is scorched and cracked open, allowing new life to emerge. Other plants hide new stems underground and the shoots won't poke above the surface until a fire has burned its way through the area.

Remissioning leaders and churches can learn to endure a fire and experience rebirth like a pyrophytic plant. I understand that wildfires are unpredictable. Wildfires cause damage. There is a risk that the fire will be too destructive and nothing will be left for a seedling to grow. But the alternative is a slow, steady decline that feels like survival but is the early stages of extinction.

Many of us hope for a grow-your-church-without-change plan. Conflict? Struggle? Death and resurrection? No, we didn't sign up for that. But established churches are much like these fire-dependent plants. Without the heat we may survive, but we won't produce fruit or multiply life.

It may feel overwhelming to think about starting the remissioning process, but the truth is you already have. Ready or not, your church is on a journey, and if you grow in awareness of your place in the life cycle, you'll have a better idea how much heat is necessary to produce new life.

Revitalization Versus Remissioning

Over the course of this book we will discuss how to remission established churches (both longstanding congregations and church plants that have survived past five years). We'll look at core competencies that aid in the remissioning process, and we'll examine practitioner-tested tools that help churches discover breakthrough in their context. But what is remissioning?

Remissioning is the process of inside-out transformation of the church through discipleship for the sake of our neighbors and world. It is a steady, purposeful, and dedicated process that involves the transformation of the leaders and church together for the sake of their community. Remissioning is much different from revitalization.

Revitalization is refreshing an existing church to do its current work with greater clarity and a goal of numerical growth. To revitalize is to work harder, smarter, and more efficiently on existing programs and events to help the church increase in relevance to the community.

Remissioning churches wrestle with a question: "If our people gathered in our building and the building fell into a sinkhole, would our community notice we were gone?" Revitalizing churches ask, "What can we do to bring more people to our programs and events?"

Revitalizing a church is like updating an app on your favorite device. Revitalization helps individual programs run more smoothly, use less battery, crash less often, and work more efficiently. Remissioning is upgrading the entire operating system so all the apps, messaging, and processes fit into a new system and work in sync with multiple other devices across the world.

Remissioning churches ask complicated questions about how to translate the gospel through life experiences, relationships, Scripture, and the Spirit who still speaks. To remission is to figure out where our church has lost the plot. Remissioning leaders recognize that our churches bear a responsibility to become Jesus-followers who go to our neighbors before asking them to come to our religious services. Questions like: Who are my neighbors? Where has the Spirit gone ahead of us? How do we catch up? To remission is to learn to repent and walk in new life for the sake of others. Remissioned churches understand that if they are thriving while their neighbors are barely surviving, then they aren't really thriving after all.

Revitalizing churches have fallen captive to the challenges named by Edwin Friedman in his essential book *A Failure of Nerve: Leadership in the Age of the Quick Fix*. They think that with a little more dedication, hard work, and a charismatic leader, their (insert the church's most popular past program or event here) will relive its glory days and the church will thrive again. But as Friedman points out, "The great lesson of this turnaround is that when any relationship system is imaginatively gridlocked, it cannot get free simply through more thinking about the problem. Conceptually stuck systems cannot become unstuck simply by trying harder."[2]

As one of my mentors, Glenn Akins, used to say, what if it worked? What if you did attract more people, grow your worship service, and revitalize your existing programs and events? How would repeating those same programs, events, and ways of being church yield different results down the road? What would suddenly cause those programs to yield different disciples?

Remissioning leaders are going on a longer journey. It's a journey of discovery, but they'll have to deal with existing issues while on the road. It's like redecking a ship while out at sea. You don't have the luxury of pulling into dock and fixing things up. You have to pull up some boards, take on some water, repair the hole, bail out the water, and then move to the next section.

One of the more familiar ways we talk about "remission" is in relation to cancer. Someone is in remission when treatments have reduced or eliminated cancer from their body. The cancer has either disappeared (complete remission) or decreased and stopped growing (partial remission). Remission requires death. The cancer cells must die for the body to live and healthy cells to grow. In a similar way, many established churches are sick, and the disease is spreading in their body, threatening their existence. To remission a church is to learn what unhealthy cells must die and seek healing for the local church body so it might live again.

Please don't misunderstand me; the church as a whole will not fail (Mt 16:18). But individual churches are regularly going into hospice care, closing their doors, and fumbling the handoff to the next generation. To focus our efforts on revitalization is to put a Band-Aid on a large wound that needs stitches and healing from the inside out. Revitalization is like receiving test results showing only partial remission and trying to convince everyone it's good enough.

To remission a church is to ask what kinds of relationships, programs, events, and shared ways of being good neighbors are necessary for God's kingdom to flourish and transform the surrounding community. This book is a field guide to remissioning established churches so they become healthy from the inside out and become good neighbors.

Outside In versus Inside Out

Established churches live on mission by creating missional outposts, planting new churches, and releasing people to create new expressions of church. They send people out on mission, which often decreases short-term conflict and releases innovative leaders to live faithfully. A revitalizing church may try to create a missional outpost in order to "live on mission," but it often struggles with the new endeavor. The established church doesn't show up to the tattoo parlor meetups, the dog park church, or the runners' club Bible study. As when established churches used to hire, fund, and send missionaries to a foreign country, revitalizing churches often send "missionaries" across town where "non-Christians" gather in hopes that eventually new converts will return to the established churches.

This outside-in approach is a challenge, because those who do meet Jesus in one of those innovative spaces or missional outposts rarely have the tolerance to attend an established church that is suspicious of their faith, judgmental of their clothes, and unsure of their character because they have no meaningful relational connection. In this approach to mission the sending church doesn't have to make sacrifices. The onus is on the new Jesus-followers to pick up on the traditions, culture, and rules of the established congregation to find community. The established church doesn't have to grow, change, or do the work; rather, it funds missionaries who do the work "out there" so members can remain safe in their enclave away from "the world."

There are many great examples of partnerships, churches supporting churches and ministries in global contexts, and empowering other parts of the body of Christ to work in their local context. However, intentional formation is necessary to break through a self-centered, survival-first approach that exports mission to others and keeps people comfortable in the sending church. These churches often struggle to make disciples who live on mission and grow in love, hospitality, and neighborliness because someone else does it for them. The sending church doesn't feel the need to change even when a trusted missionary tries to bring a new person into the fold. This methodology has gotten us into our current predicament where the average church size is shrinking, dying churches are outpacing new church starts, and mistrust of pastors and churches is at an all-time high.[3]

However, it's not all bad news. Churches around the world are taking the invitation to love their neighbors and make disciples seriously and experiencing breakthrough as they learn to grow mission from within their church for the sake of their neighbors. One remissioning church located in a highly transitional community near a military base began a new program with well-trained volunteers and thorough background checks to offer free childcare one night a week so parents who had moved away from their families could attend to their marriage, rest, have fun, or run errands. They recognized that they could create a sense of home away from home and learned to love their neighbors without asking anything in return. It turns out that when people are served in practical ways and you care for their children, they are inspired to worship, join a discipleship group, and make friends with the church. The changes the church needed to make in their worship times, dress code, and budget occurred with minimal conflict because their hearts were changed to love their neighbors over prioritizing their own preferences.

Another remissioning congregation in the UK sold its existing building and partnered with the local government to create a school that would also serve as a worship space on the weekend. The church provided volunteers throughout the school, shared the building space weekly, and invested in the lives of families in the community. Instead of asking the community to adjust to the congregation's building needs, they made tangible sacrifices to serve their neighbors. As a result the church became a hub for community engagement and support. Did it make the life of the church easier to set up and break down each week for worship? Did it simplify the organizational structure to coordinate safeguarding practices and serve on the board of directors to share the space? Of course not. But as the church grew to love the students and their families, the extra work to coordinate with local government became a powerful example to the neighborhood of how a church can invest in the good of the community.

Remissioning churches aim to grow transformational disciples from the inside out who will imitate Jesus and seek the flourishing of their neighbors. It's a slower process than revitalization, but it helps reduce the false notion that we can export mission to someone else to do on our behalf. As the good doctor and amazing missiologist Eun Strawser says in the quote to start this chapter, the mission of God isn't meant for just some of us; it's an invitation and challenge for all of us.

GROWING UP AND GROWING OUT

I grew up as a pastor's kid living up and down the East Coast. I moved a lot and went to three different middle schools in two states in three years. Because of all the moves, church was one of the places where I clung to relationships. I spent the first half of my childhood in established, traditional churches. Despite their traditionalism, I was fortunate to know people across generations, from different socioeconomic contexts and cultural experiences, who live on purpose with one another and take big leaps to live on mission in ways that made them uncomfortable yet committed to creating disciples. The second half of my childhood was in a church plant that never owned its own building. The church plant was committed to living on mission in both a local and global context, and it wrestled constantly with how to be relevant and attract new people while acknowledging that events and fun programming couldn't replace meaningful relationships.

In college I worked on staff with a nonprofit that practiced incarnational outreach to middle school and high school students, meeting them in their context rather than urging them to enter a church building. After graduation I went on staff at a church plant where I spent the next eleven years. I worked with students, managed communications, preached, taught at a local seminary, and led in various denominational networks.

Much to my surprise, while I was researching how churches, businesses, and nonprofits experience change and leaders bring people through the change process, I was invited to take my theories out of the abstract and put them into practice as the senior pastor of a congregation that described itself as stuck and unsure how to experience new life together.

Over the last ten years these theories, principles, and tools have moved from theoretical into real practice in my local congregation and have been used in churches across the United States, the United Kingdom, and a few other countries. These churches have gone on remissioning journeys with me, along with a team of coaches committed to the process. I'm passionate about remissioning. Empowering stuck, struggling, and dying churches to discover new life on the other side of pain can create a transition from selfishness to generosity so that congregations become assets to their communities instead of liabilities.

My remissioning journey with churches is like the old "Hair Club for Men" commercials from my childhood. The president would say at the end of the ad: "I'm not just the president; I'm also a client." The tools, frameworks, and stories are born out of my serving with two churches over twenty years. After all this time pastoring, I am more hopeful for the church today than when I first started. I've seen bridges between previously disconnected communities built. Intergenerational hubs of mission created. People who were disillusioned put their heart into meaningful community service and begin worshiping again.

Over the course of this book, we'll explore some of the markers of maturity in the remissioning process (learning to embrace change *before* plateau instead of waiting for decline, dropout, and dysfunction), as well as how to lead a church through this process. My hope is that we'll continue to grow a movement of churches and leaders willing to do the death-and-new-life work that unleashes the power of the resurrection in our local communities so we can experience a mutual transformation through relationships, justice, and grace.

These are the core competences we'll look at:

- Being a disciple
- Creative destruction
- Traditioned innovation
- Discipleship pathways
- Remissioning leadership

As we unpack these core remissioning skills, we'll also deploy a number of tested tools to help us put these skills into practice in our communities (both with church and neighbors). These tools will help you do the following:

- Exegete your church and community
- Prune for new life
- Lead through change
- Identify gaps
- Grow intercultural intelligence
- Begin with the end
- Remember well
- Create shared experiments
- Structure for mission
- Embrace conflict
- Develop healthy metrics
- Identify your church on the life cycle

After working with churches across various denominational, ethnic, and international contexts, I've found these tools and skills to aid in the remissioning journey guided by the grace of the Spirit.

FURTHER READING

E. K. Strawser, *Centering Discipleship: A Pathway for Multiplying Spectators into Mature Disciples* (Downers Grove, IL: InterVarsity Press, 2023).

Edwin Friedman, *A Failure of Nerve: Leadership in the Age of the Quick Fix* (New York: Seabury Books, 2007).

Phyllis Tickle, *The Great Emergence* (Grand Rapids, MI: Baker Books, 2012).

2

REMISSIONING THROUGH DESCENT

I am telling you all this because I am deeply convinced that the Christian leader of the future is called to be completely irrelevant and to stand in this world with nothing to offer but his or her own vulnerable self. That is the way Jesus came to reveal God's love. The great message that we have to carry, as ministers of God's Word and followers of Jesus, is that God loves us not because of what we do or accomplish, but because God has created and redeemed us in love and has chosen us to proclaim that love as the true source of all human life.

HENRI NOUWEN, *IN THE NAME OF JESUS*

I HAD TO BUY FOUR SUITS to start my first job at an established church. Leaving the church plant I had served at for eleven years to pastor a church that was 157 years old required a different wardrobe. On the surface putting on a suit and tie is no big deal. They cost a few hundred bucks, and it was a small sacrifice to make for the job change.

But those suits were cloth monuments to a deeper truth: the changes on the outside were nothing compared to the transformation required within. The suits were soft reminders each week of the temptations so easy to succumb to as a pastor: to be seen as someone who was relevant, popular, and worthy of leading—all idols that needed to be buried. Trading jeans, boots, and an unbuttoned collar for striped ties, loafers, and four suits (navy, brown, charcoal, and black) was a gentle reminder that from the surface all the way into the depths of my heart, remissioning would require transformation of my own soul—not just changes for "them." Remissioning an established church has required me to reflect on and repent from chasing after idols. This process will also implore you to discover, bury, and leave behind your own temptations, preferences, and vain images so you might experience transformation too.

Leaders May Eat Last but Also Go First

Transformation of an established church requires transformation of the leader (usually before transformation can happen in the congregation). Simon Sinek wrote *Leaders Eat Last* as a testament to leaders who empower others instead of drawing attention and power to themselves.[1] Remissioning leaders will indeed need to eat last, but they will also have to go first in demonstrating the sacrificial cost of transformation. Images in our head must be transformed. The emphasis must shift from stages and bright lights to slow conversations and coffee tables.

The Spirit is inviting established churches into a new future. Yet it is tempting to focus on the problems they must tackle (organizational ruts, historical barriers, institutional mistrust, mission drift) and then start throwing quick fixes at the wall hoping to simply survive. Hoping something will finally stick. The reality is, the Spirit is waking up established churches to do much more than barely exist—the Spirit is helping them learn how to thrive and make disciples again. The invitation set before established churches is to recalibrate our existence around missional presence and the flourishing of our neighborhoods. To do this the church needs remissioners.

Remissioners are people called by the Spirit to embrace movemental ecclesiology and reproducible discipleship. Remissioners help churches to wake up from their theological, spiritual, and emotional slumber into a new day. Remissioners help established churches learn to lose their lives so they might find them again. But first, remissioners must be disciples themselves, losing their life to truly find it.

The Up, In, and Out of Following Jesus

Leading an established church takes disciples through a familiar three-part movement. There is an upward, inward, and outward journey that helps us find communion with God, belonging with other Jesus-followers, and transformation with our neighbors for the good of our community.

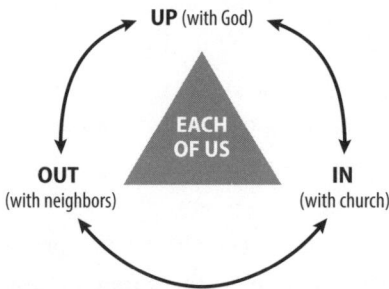

Figure 2.1. The up, in, and out of following Jesus

The upward journey is the path where we grow our in our communion with God. We learn from the Psalms how to pray in times of great flourishing and times of great pain. When the well feels dry or a season of winter is upon us, how do we continue to struggle and relate to God? When the well is full and the harvest in plentiful, how do we celebrate God's goodness? How do we practice the presence of God in our lives? The remissioning journey can be difficult, and without regular communion with God, it will be difficult to sustain.

Remissioning will bring times of pain, betrayal, and heartache. How do we bring the pain of our lives to Jesus? When we suffer as leaders, friends, parents, and humans, how do we bring our suffering to Jesus? How do we create space for God to heal our hurt through his generous love?

The inward journey is about how we are formed in the context of Christian community. This part of the journey asks us to be honest with ourselves about our own imperfections as leaders, friends, pastors, and followers of Jesus in light of our relationships in the church. Who are the people who truly know us? Remissioning is a sending journey that is disinterested in creating Christian cul-de-sacs of relationships, and it can be tempting to hide in plain view and not live our faith with other Jesus-followers who can provide accountability, challenge, and deep invitation. To be a disciple is to imitate Jesus with other imitators and fellow sojourners on the path.

This inward journey is also marked by a growing self-awareness and commitment to community. There are places of brokenness in each of us. What things make us weak and present challenges in leading and serving others? Is it the need to be right? To be in control? To have a shiny image that masks our imperfections or vulnerabilities? Do we avoid conflict at all cost? Do we lose our own perspective when there are many perspectives in the room? How do we treat our enemies or people who challenge us in our faith community? Our inward journey with other Jesus-followers helps us practice a more mature hospitality when we live in community with our neighbors.

Often the wounds we bear below the surface stem from trauma, past family experiences, and painful church relationships, and sometimes those wounds lead us to wound others. The inward journey helps us discover both the ways we hurt others and the ways we have been hurt by others so we might move toward one another in forgiveness and reconciliation. How do we remain faithful to confess our brokenness and woundedness in our context?

The outward journey is how we join in the mission of God as our hopes and fears, joys and insecurities, order and chaos are revealed to us as we seek the flourishing of our world. As in every other aspect of remissioning, "God's Spirit wants to take us on a journey of discovery and transformation."[2] What things within us make it a challenge to live out our faith in our local community? What things do we discover as we meet people who are suspicious of our faith?

Notice that the outward journey isn't *for* or *to* our neighbors. This journey is *with* our neighbors. We often want to create separation or hierarchy rooted in unhelpful power dynamics, as though we were somehow above our neighbors. To be on a remissioning journey is to recognize that our experiences, relationships, and shared humanity with our neighbors is one of the primary ways God disrupts our vain plans of rescuing people.

It is essential that each of us go on these journeys of up, in, and out so we can point people to Jesus rather than ourselves. Henri Nouwen sums this up well:

> We are not the healers, we are not the reconcilers, we are not the givers of life. We are sinful, broken, vulnerable people who need as much care as anyone we care for. The mystery of ministry is that we have been chosen to make our own limited and very conditional love the gateway for the unlimited and unconditional love of God. Therefore, true ministry must be mutual. When the members of a community of faith cannot truly know and love their shepherd, shepherding quickly becomes a subtle way of exercising power over others and begins to show authoritarian and dictatorial traits.[3]

Remissioning established churches requires the transformation of leaders who are willing to go on a journey of discovery, repentance, and resurrection in their relationship with God, Christian community, and neighbors. And this willingness to be transformed will help point ourselves, our fellow disciples, and our neighbors to the One whose love never runs out.

THE JOURNEY OF DESCENT

To remission churches, leaders need to learn how to cultivate a spirituality of weakness. A spirituality of weakness is rooted in the self-emptying (or *kenōsis* in the Greek) embodied by Jesus in the incarnation. Paul brings this to life in Philippians 2:

> Therefore if you have any encouragement from being united with Christ, if any comfort from his love, if any common sharing in the Spirit, if any tenderness and compassion, then make my joy complete by being like-minded, having the same love, being one in spirit and of one mind. Do nothing out of selfish ambition or vain conceit. Rather, in humility value others above yourselves, not looking to your own interests but each of you to the interests of the others.
>
> In your relationships with one another, have the same mindset as Christ Jesus:
>
> Who, being in very nature God,
> did not consider equality with God something to be used to his
> own advantage;
> rather, he made himself nothing
> by taking the very nature of a servant,
> being made in human likeness.
> And being found in appearance as a man,
> he humbled himself
> by becoming obedient to death—
> even death on a cross! (Phil 2:1-8)

Do me a favor. Read that passage one more time. If there is an overarching text that helps us reflect on what remissioning a church will require, this is it.

In verse seven, Paul says Jesus "made himself nothing," emptied himself, becoming like a servant. This self-emptying led Jesus toward people; it was a descent from the usual way of wielding power, and then it compelled Jesus outward in service.

The move toward others is complemented by a descent, where the lordship of Jesus is not something used to his own advantage, but instead is emptied out as Jesus takes the form of a servant. Jesus is looking for the hopes and interests of others while laying down his own preferences for power or control.

AVOIDING THE SHAME GAME

Over the course of the remissioning journey you may feel ashamed. Ashamed for your church in the ways they have failed to love their neighbors, ashamed for their stubbornness and multiple adventures in missing the point. You'll feel ashamed when your blind spots become apparent to you and you realize you have wasted time, missed neighbors, and focused on growing programs instead of discipling people. You may feel ashamed in comparison to other pastors and churches. When you experience shame you may be tempted to get stuck in the embarrassment and isolation it creates within us.

Brené Brown says, "Shame is the intensely painful feeling or experience of believing that we are flawed and therefore unworthy of love, belonging and connection."[4]

The invitation to remission through descent isn't an invitation to get stuck in the shame that comes through learning to see ourselves and our neighbors. The journey of descent is an invitation and challenge to break the cycle of shame, guilt, and brokenness that often keeps us from cross-informed vulnerability so we can stop scapegoating one another and find freedom in the mission of God together.

In my early thirties I went to a public gathering in Richmond, Virginia, with other pastors to publicly lament and pray over the atrocities in Charlottesville after white supremacists had surrounded churches, driven a car into protesters, and terrified a community. I had only recently started working at an established church. I wasn't sure of the dress code for an event like this, so I arrived at the public vigil in one of those four new suits I had just purchased. Most of the other church-plant pastors looked like they'd stepped out of an Urban Outfitters advertisement. The only other people in suits were pastors and leaders of established congregations, and most had more than a few years of seniority on me.

I felt like an outsider among my peers. I was new to the region. It was one of the first times I could clearly see the differences between my church-planting days and leadership of an established church. Then I felt shame for being worried about my appearance amid the real reason for the gathering. Comparison is a thief to mission. Being uncomfortable in my clothes was a minimal cost when praying and seeking justice.

The aim of remissioning work isn't to grow a profound awareness in the pastor or leaders so they can berate and dominate their congregants into a submissive posture of mission. The aim of remissioning is to liberate our congregations from the idols of power, control, exclusion, and domination so they can taste the sweet freedom that happens through the life, death, and resurrection of Jesus. This freedom in Christ eliminates the need to perpetuate systems that are more interested in who gets the last word than shared leadership. The descending Jesus frees people to come along on the journey instead of racing to be first. This liberation reduces our shame so churches and neighbors can find wholeness together in the One whose love never runs out.

Before a leader or church can experience resurrection, there is descent, struggle, death, waiting, and then new life. How can your leadership model the journey with your church so it might reawaken to mission again?

FURTHER READING

Brené Brown, *Atlas of the Heart* (New York: Random House, 2021).

Henri Nouwen, *In the Name of Jesus* (New York: Crossroad Company, 1989).

Howard Thurman, *Jesus and the Disinherited* (Boston: Beacon, 1996).

Peter Scazzero, *The Emotionally Healthy Church: A Strategy for Discipleship that Actually Changes Lives* (Grand Rapids, MI: Zondervan, 2017).

3

FINDING OURSELVES IN
THE REMISSIONING STORY

*When we choose to incarnate, we hang between our own world and
the world of another person. We are called to remain faithful to
who we are, not losing our essence, while at the same time entering
into the world of another. We can be assured, however, that as Jesus'
incarnation and death brought great life, so our choice to do the same
will also result in resurrection life and much fruit in us and others.*

PETER SCAZZERO, *THE EMOTIONALLY HEALTHY CHURCH*

when you come to the realization
that God has always been for them
whoever them *is*
you will hear the sound of chains breaking

DREW JACKSON, *GOD SPEAKS THROUGH WOMBS*

THEY SAY IT'S EASIER to birth a baby than to raise the dead.

You can't teach an old dog new tricks.

Don't change anything for two years.

These are some of the proverbs shared with me about the dangers, risks,
and struggles in remissioning a church.

I had a season where I served in a local association of churches by helping run gatherings of youth pastors, organizing youth retreats, and facilitating learning groups with other emerging leaders. A large group of us were working on a creative project together when one of the larger churches pulled their funding and participation out of the blue. It was tough. I talked with the association leader about how to find creative solutions to keep the event from failing. After five years of serving on various teams and committees, I was told by the association leader that if I wanted to do creative work, "something out of the box," I needed to leave the association and denomination. Things wouldn't ever change, so I should stop trying.

Is this really the truth about what it means to be an established church? Is this the best we have to offer? Is this the end game for every church—people don't change and so neither will churches?

I've heard that if you can't remission a church, just start a new one! But the pain of our experiences doesn't disappear when we move on without processing the hurt. The last thing church plants need is wounded remissioners who leak the pain and despair of their last environment onto a new group of folks.

When I left a church plant to remission an established church, most people talked to me about the impossibility of transformation in existing churches—or at least that transformation from the inside out is too much work with too little reward, so it's mostly futile.

There is a story that gets to the heart of what remissioning is like in Luke's Gospel. In Luke 8:40-56, Jesus is approached by Jairus, a synagogue leader who falls at Jesus' feet, pleads with him to come to his house, and begs for help because his only daughter is dying. Jesus agrees, and on the way large crowds press in all around Jesus and the disciples. The crowd is so large it almost crushes them. A woman who has had uncontrolled bleeding for twelve years comes up to Jesus, touches his cloak, and is healed. Jesus senses that power has left him and asks his disciples to help find the person who was healed. The woman, who'd hoped to blend back into the crowd, comes trembling to Jesus' feet and tells him how she was healed. Jesus acknowledges her tenderly and sends her off in peace.

While Jesus has paused the journey to Jairus's house, Jairus's daughter dies. Family and friends tell Jesus not to worry about coming to the house anymore, but Jesus still goes. When he arrives, he says the girl is not dead but asleep, and the crowd laughs and mocks him. Meanwhile, Jesus goes with Peter, James, and John up to the room where the girl has died and brings her back to life. No one can believe what has happened.

In this story there are three connections to remissioning that are important for us to consider: power, interruption, and ridicule. Established churches are filled with power dynamics, interruptions (both perceived and real), and disbelief in the ability of people to change. Let's take a closer look at each.

POWER

In this story a religious leader has unwittingly created a trap for Jesus. Jairus has gathered with a crowd to beg for Jesus' help and invite him to his home to heal his only daughter. This isn't an even playing field. Jairus is a synagogue leader. A community organizer. A person with power. And he falls at Jesus' feet, pleading for help. What is Jesus to do?

The implications of Jesus' response to this leader in these circumstances apply to us in our work with established churches today. What can we learn from his interactions with Jairus about our own relationship with power? In remissioning churches there are many complicated relationships, and leaders usually avoid, challenge, or accept the power dynamics.

It is unhelpful to simply avoid engaging with power dynamics. To do so is to ignore the way past leadership has formed the people in your congregation. Simply ignoring the dynamics doesn't mean the issues will go away on their own. People have been formed over time by leaders and their discipleship pathways, so to pretend they don't exist doesn't change anything. You can avoid for a season, but that won't make the problem go away or create change.

Challenging and accepting the power dynamics are two sides of the same coin. In remissioning a church, you will find there are times to challenge and times to accept. Accepting power dynamics can be a form of complacency and avoidance if the goal is to minimize the possibility of conflict. However, accepting the power dynamics so you can engage with people where they are, honoring their position of leadership and working through that relationship, is one of the ways you grow trust and disciple people.

Leading in an established church requires intentional examination of the power dynamics in your context. Practicing a spirituality of weakness doesn't mean you are devoid of power. It means you submit the authority, role, and office of your leadership to a mission larger than yourself. Unlike those who seek control, authority, and elevation of themselves above others, leaders in a remissioning situation seek something greater than power as an end in itself. Power is to be engaged so the larger mission can come into focus and be pursued.

Where do people with power in your context go to seek healing and transformation? What power dynamics seem unhealthy in your context? Where are power and authority being wielded well? Does your church tend to elevate loud leaders who are emotionally, spiritually, or relationally dysfunctional? Does your church tend to bring young and culturally intelligent people into leadership? Are there leaders in your context like Jairus, begging for healing, hoping their children will find hope and life again?

Even in healthy environments, power is something you must pay attention to and cultivate well with great intention. As you think about the story of Jairus, which character do you relate to in terms of power dynamics? What is your normal response to power? Do you tend to avoid, accept, or challenge?

One remissioning leader I know could clearly articulate the problems his church was facing, but when it came to raising the issues to his leadership team, he couldn't get the words out. The pastor wanted things to improve, but he avoided naming the ways he saw the church treating new guests in worship—with disdain. For many remissioning leaders, naming truth to power is a recipe for avoidance. Knowing this about ourselves can help us to create strategies to grow. One of my suggestions to this leader was to write things down ahead of time so he didn't feel like he had to have it all memorized. Make notes of key points to use as a reference throughout the conversation.

It is fundamentally important to pay attention to the way power dynamics are at work inside your church, because your neighbors are also paying attention. They're taking note of the way you do these things:

- protect children and handle situations of abuse
- navigate conflict

- describe issues of culture, race, class, and justice
- love people who are different from the majority culture of your church
- disagree with each other politically
- engage with power in the community

INTERRUPTIONS

In the middle of the journey to heal Jairus's daughter, a woman who has had medical issues that would isolate her from religious community and complicate her relationship with faith comes to Jesus, touches the edge of his cloak, and is healed. Jesus could have continued the journey and ignored the interruption, but instead he stops and seeks out the woman.

Jesus' disciples think he's crazy, but Jesus remains steady in his desire to find the woman. The woman realizes she is going to be found out, and she (like Jairus) falls at Jesus' feet. In the presence of the crowd she describes how she has been healed. Jesus calls her "daughter" and tells her to go in peace. What is an interruption for Jairus is a moment of healing for this unnamed woman.

In remissioning work, the goal can often be to create a more productive and efficient system, one that doesn't include the interruptions inherent with working with people and navigating the messy parts of life. It can be tempting for us to elevate efficiency to the point that unnamed people in our community are not seen or given attention.

How can we learn to be present in the interruptions and even grow to see interruptions as part of the work itself? I learned this lesson the hard way. I was late to almost every meeting during my first six months at an established church. Why? I didn't plan enough time to walk out of my office to another room or to my car. I could get to my car and most places in the building within a one-minute walk—if I kept my head down, avoided eye contact, and ignored the "Hey, Pastor Josh!" from the kids in our childcare center, our front desk volunteers (and their friends), and neighbors who'd stopped by looking for some food to make it through until the weekend. It took me a while to realize I needed to build an extra ten minutes into my "commute" so I could pay attention to the people in my path that day.

Are there people who are "interruptions" to your church, who have touched the cloak but whom you've simply passed by without stopping to see, touch, or heal? Who are the people in your life that you choose to ignore when they come by for healing? In connecting the story of the woman in the crowd to the importance of developing a spirituality of weakness, what people in your life are easiest for you to ignore?

Henri Nouwen was walking with a professor and mentor complaining about interruptions from students and people when his mentor shared, "You know . . . my whole life I have been complaining that my work was constantly interrupted, until I discovered that my interruptions were my work."[1] What does it look like to be present with those who feel like an interruption to your mission?

What about the interruptions to your life when you are with family? With friends? Do you have enough margin when life happens and gets complicated to be present? Are there leaders in your church helping to protect your time, heart, and relationships?

RIDICULE

After this interruption, Jesus is finally approaching Jairus's house when someone comes to find him and report that Jairus's daughter is already dead. They are too late. Jesus claims that she is not dead, and the people should believe! When he arrives at the home, he brings his three closest disciples and the child's parents and says she is not dead but asleep—and the crowd laughs at him. Jesus doesn't give up but grabs her by the hand and says, "Child, get up!" And the young girl gets up and eats. Her parents are astonished.

When you talk about remissioning and let folks know what you are considering, do you find that people respond like the crowd at Jairus's home? Do people think you are naive as you share your heart about helping your established church wake up to mission? When you think about the voice in your own head, what do you hear when you consider the remissioning journey? Do you have your own internal crowd casting doubt on your calling and work?

Pause for a moment here. Find a place of stillness and be honest with yourself. Where do you find yourself today or in this season when it comes to believing remissioning is possible? Where is your church in believing remissioning is possible for themselves? Do you resonate with the crowd laughing at Jesus' announcement that Jairus's dead daughter is alive? Or do you feel like Jairus and the disciples, along for the ride but having no clue what's about to happen? Do you sense a clear call to help remission your church from the inside out?

There is room for you to be in any of those spaces. There is no judgment. But movement requires honesty. And how we handle ridicule from others—or the voice in our own head—matters.

HOPE

When it comes to working with churches, they say it's easier to birth a baby than to raise the dead. If we think the work of remissioning is about our own power and effort, then this might be true. But is it true for Jesus? Can't Jesus say "Get up!" to our churches?

The false narrative that it's easier to plant churches than to remission established churches doesn't take seriously the incredible challenge and gift it is to plant. And the false narrative that established churches can't remission dismisses the very heartbeat of the gospel: people can change! Life can be found in death! The last, least, and most unlikely of places is where God often shows up.

The kind of hope we are talking about in remissioning isn't easy or cheap. Jairus's daughter died. It was heartbreaking. Hope seemed like a distant galaxy far, far away. To be faithful to this calling to remission means you as a leader will need to be honest with yourself (and, over time, with your church leaders, friends, and family) about the power, interruptions, and ridicule that you will face.

The good news is that God is in the raising-the-dead line of work. The tough news is that some things will have to die for them to be raised to new life. Where do you find yourself in this story?

4

REMISSIONERS SHIFT FROM OWNERSHIP TO STEWARDSHIP

The man who stores up injuries and resentments and yet fancies that he prays might as well draw water from a well and pour it into a cask that is full of holes.

EVAGRIUS PONTICUS, *THE PRAKTIKOS AND CHAPTERS ON PRAYER*

IT IS NOT POSSIBLE FOR YOU to separate your emotional and spiritual health as a leader in the remissioning process.

For far too long we have made Christianity something that changes our minds but has little effect on our bodies. The longer we press into the remissioning process, the more we see that it's impossible to profess love for Jesus with our mind but treat ourselves, our neighbors, our spouse, our friends, or our children like garbage. If the way we think doesn't impact the way we live, we need a major course correction.

SELF-CARE AND SUSTAINABLE PRACTICES

Self-care and sustainable practices are about creating a rule of life. This concept comes from early Christians who were incredibly intentional to order their spiritual lives in a way that created the best environment for their faith to grow.

Don't be intimidated by the word *rule*. It comes from the Greek word for "trellis." In a garden, for a tomato plant to produce healthy and abundant fruit, it needs support. It needs a trellis. The plant grows around this structure, which then supports the plant and helps bear the weight of the fruit as it matures. A trellis is a tool that helps the tomato plant to grow upward and be more fruitful and productive.

In the same way, a rule of life is a trellis that helps us situate our lives in Christ and become more fruitful spiritually and relationally. A rule of life is an intentional, conscious plan to keep God at the center of everything we do. It helps us practice keeping the presence of God in front of us and behind us and remembering God as the source of our everyday life. A rule of life is a collection of practices that helps provide structure and direction for us to pay attention and live with God in everything we do. The starting point, foundation, and aim of a rule of life is to grow our desire to be with God and to love Jesus.

The reality is, however, that few of us have a conscious plan for developing our spiritual lives. It is easy for us to not be intentional but to be functional, like cars driving down the road in cruise control. Our crammed schedules, endless to-do lists, demanding jobs and families, constant noise, twenty-four-hour news, anxiety, and undealt-with grief can make us speed up instead of slowing down to be with God.

We have all kinds of routines that manage our lives. I bet when you wake up you have a routine, don't you? Maybe you wake up, feed the cat, make coffee, exercise, get dressed for the day, and eat breakfast. You have a trellis for your spiritual life too. It may include worship on Sunday, Sunday school, small group involvement, serving somewhere, and ten minutes of reading Scripture or praying before going to bed.

For most of us, our spiritual practices are not enough to keep us afloat in the ocean of modern life. More often than not, regardless of age, I find people saying they feel unfocused, distracted, and spiritually adrift. Having a trellis that can support the weight of remissioning is another demand altogether.

In fact, people in churches often live off others' spirituality instead of developing their own direct experience with God. Many Christians talk about prayer but don't pray. Many Christians talk about the Bible as the Word of God but have very little idea what it says. We talk about wanting future generations to carry on the faith, but we put the most attention on education, wealth, beauty, and popularity. In contrast, following Jesus is the following:

- relational (not simple attendance with a disconnected heart)
- personal (beyond the platitudes we see on TV or social media)
- communal (not individualistic; it's more than "me and Jesus")
- everyday (not just on days with scheduled religious activities)
- a blend of faith and works (not talk without action)
- a balanced diet (not a buffet where you eat everything you want with no consequences)
- costly (it takes time)
- grace-filled (you don't have to earn it, and God is faithful)

It is tempting to avoid this conversation. But everywhere we look we are being encouraged to move further and further away from one another. In this cultural climate where it is so hard to have healthy, positive, respectful conversations rooted in common language and trust, how are we to follow Jesus?

PLAN, THEN BUILD

Jesus tells this story in Luke 14:28-30: "Suppose one of you wants to build a tower. Won't you first sit down and estimate the cost to see if you have enough money to complete it? For if you lay the foundation and are not able to finish it, everyone who sees it will ridicule you, saying, 'This person began to build and wasn't able to finish.'"

If you lay a foundation but aren't able to finish the building project, everyone who sees it will wonder about your maturity and your planning. Why did you begin if you couldn't finish the job? As one of my mentors told me, "It's not good to have unfinished chapters in your life."[1]

Remissioning an established church is among the most difficult work a pastor can be called to today. To plan and build the tower is to put practices in place that help us have healthy relationships and grow our faith amid the grief, pain, challenges, and difficulties of the journey. To have self-care means we will be intentional about sustainable practices that help us integrate our emotional and spiritual lives and give ourselves the best opportunities to flourish. Table 4.1 includes some categories we can use to create our rule-of-life trellis.

Table 4.1. Remissioning rule of life

Spiritual Practices	Rest
1. Scripture	1. Sabbath
2. Silence and solitude	2. Simplicity
3. Daily Office	3. Play and fun
4. Prayer	
5. Study	
Relationships	**Work**
1. Emotional health	1. Service and mission
2. Family	2. Care for physical body
3. Community	3. Care for home
4. Friends	

I'd like to invite you to create your own chart. Here are some simple insights that can help you as you plan:

- *Think simply.* Don't overcomplicate this. Start with practices that help you connect with God. Not everything should be a struggle, but list at least one practice that helps you stretch.

- *Name a specific practice.* My chart includes broad categories, but get granular with yours. For Scripture, list something like, "Read through the Psalms." For play and fun, name a specific practice, such as "Play golf," "Go hiking," or "Watch soccer."

- *Who will you practice with?* If this is a solo endeavor, name it. If it's a practice you plan to share with friends or family, name that too!

- *How often will you practice?* Daily, weekly, monthly, quarterly? Some practices can't be done each week, while others need daily attention. Be as specific as you can to give yourself the best opportunity to be intentional.

We live into spiritual, emotional, relational, and missional health one trellis rung at a time. God has more than enough resources to help your faith grow and to sustain you in this work. His resources empower you to grow and to be fruitful, but you will need to count the cost. Finding support reinforces our life trellis and helps us stay rooted in the love and hope of God—who also counted the cost in building a relational tower with us so we can know we are seen, loved, and invited to grow.

For reference, table 4.2 is an example of my rule of life.

Table 4.2. Josh Hayden's rule of life

Spiritual practices	Rest
1. Read through the canonical Scriptures plus Psalms each day using The Bible Project over the course of one year. 2. Practice silence twice a week. 3. Reach out to one person each day who I am praying for.	1. Rest half of Friday into half of Saturday each week. 2. Watch at least one soccer game each month; explore one new restaurant a month with someone in my family or a friend.
Relationships	**Work**
1. See a therapist monthly. 2. Schedule regular administrative discussions and meet regularly with each child; plan regular rest and friendship time with spouse. 3. At least once a month gather for fun with people. 4. Meet a friend for lunch (not connected to work) each month.	1. Find one way to serve in the community that doesn't benefit the church. 2. Run or exercise four times each week. 3. Coordinate home project schedule and plan with family.

Slowing Down, Paying Attention, and Living with Integrity

One of the worst things we can do as remissioners is perpetuate something from the pulpit, from the platform of our lives, that we don't live out in our own relationships. The thing about remissioning is that you have to throw a lot of spaghetti at the wall to see what sticks. It's a busy work for the first five years. A lot of experimentation, struggle, fun, loss, and conversation. Sometimes we can end up being busy about the wrong things.

We struggle to cultivate and nourish a rich interior life with God. As Peter Scazzero says in *The Emotionally Healthy Church*, "Work for God that is not nourished by a deep interior life with God will eventually be contaminated. Our experiential sense of worth and validation gradually shifts from God's love for us in Christ to our works and performance. The joy of life with Christ slowly, almost imperceptibly, disappears."[2]

If we don't slow down, we may completely miss out on the thing that is most important. When Martha says to Jesus, "Lord, don't you care that my sister has left me to do the work by myself? Tell her to help me!" Jesus responds, "Martha, you are worried and upset about many things, but few things are needed—or indeed only one" (Lk 10:40-42).

To slow down and live with integrity does *not* mean you don't accomplish any more tasks once you follow Jesus. It means you get your priorities in order. Remissioning will have seasons of deep intensity that you cannot outlast on your own. You can try to ignore what's happening in the deeper parts of your life, but you will circle back again and again around the same core relational issues without seeing growth. Slowing down is a direct affront to the incessant need to achieve, do work, and pretend we don't really need God. Slowing down is a regular reminder that we aren't God and we aren't in control. Slowing down and paying attention helps us to live with integrity.

Integrity means we have to be honest about the broken places of our lives that destroy and hurt us and the people closest to us. God doesn't cause disorienting events and experiences to happen to us, but in God's grace he doesn't waste the pain. God is very interested in our hearts growing larger. Scazzero says it like this: "Every spiritual journey takes us to the hardest realities in our lives, the monsters within us, our shadows and strongholds, our willful flesh, and our inner demons. It is essential that we understand these enemies within us or we will inevitably project them outward on to other people."[3]

If we aren't careful, we can become addicted to our busyness, like we are addicted to technology, and we can never get off the adrenaline and slow down. We live in fear that if we slow down one step, things will certainly fall apart. It is impossible to live with integrity without reflection on why we do what we do. One of my own greatest fears coming out of an intense season of remissioning was: could my body, heart, and mind realign after living in deep intensity without living in dread that another shoe might drop?

At the heart of this principle, to slow down and live with integrity, is the willingness to avoid using busyness as a mask for pain, shortcomings, or an inability to handle joy or a way to ignore the hurt someone has hoisted upon you as their pastor or leader. So, instead of ignoring the pain, use it as a way to be open before God and allow God to reveal to you in prayer, in quiet, without "achieving" anything, that you are loved and have nothing else to prove.

You develop self-care and sustainable practices not because you will be perfect. You develop a trellis for your life because you are loved by Jesus in all your doing and your being and you have nothing left to prove. Which leads us to an important perspective shift in our life as leader of a church: from ownership to stewardship.

From Ownership to Stewardship

Letting go of the need to possess, originate, dictate, and be in charge of everything is a core part of the remissioning process. And it begins with self-aware leaders who can recognize the temptation in their own lives and the churches they serve. Too often we begin remissioning by taking the magnifying glass to our congregations and looking for the programs that have run their course, sacred traditions that need to be melted down, or toxic people who need to be discipled or encouraged to move on.

From control to vulnerability. The movement from ownership to stewardship is a shift from control to vulnerability. Remissioning requires church leaders to let go of the illusion that they are in control and the church is "theirs." Ownership says, "This is mine and I will protect it and my investment at all costs." Stewardship says, "I will tend to it, care for it, and think about its long-term fruitfulness beyond my control."

This shift is highlighted in the book *Who Stole My Church?* by Gordon MacDonald.[4] Somewhere along the line we have confused leadership with ownership. Remissioning a church requires the leader and the people to understand that the answer to this question is always: no one—it's not your church in the first place.

Not yours in the first place. The first year I had a garden, I was meticulous with details. I bought a book that helped me plan which plants grew best in proximity together, how deep to plant the seeds, how long germination would take, how to limit the number of weeds, and how much water the plants needed to grow.

For months I watched as the plants grew. I followed instructions. I paid close attention to the leaves and the fruit and crops that were produced. I celebrated when I had enough tomatoes, onions, and cilantro to make salsa. Corn took the longest to grow, but it grew. The stalks were healthy and the corn was coming in ripe. The evening before I was going to pick the corn, I stood back and was proud of my work. I gave thanks for how my hands had gotten the soil ready and my watering had helped the plant grow tall, how my attention helped the stalks be fertile and produce ears of corn. I came down the next morning, eager to harvest my crop, only to see that the deer and raccoons had a similar sense of timing. Their footprints were evident among traces of the bountiful corn harvest they had enjoyed while I slept.

For much of that day I considered learning how to hunt. All of that work—months and months of work, attention, care, water; I even sang to those stalks of corn!—only to have them snatched up by wild animals.

My little garden plot in a big forty-acre field wasn't really "mine." I was stewarding a little portion of that field animals of all types called home. When we are leading a church (and this isn't just a message to lead pastors), we can easily become confused about who the field, crop, and workers of this church garden really belong to. Dan White Jr. says:

> I call ministry leadership "the great squeeze." Under great pressure stuff comes out of our soul that we'd like to ignore. . . . There is nothing like the close proximity of people and the unspoken expectations from within and without to put a vice grip on our character. My own soul has toxic matter sloshing around that, placed under the right weight, heat, demands and ambitions, starts to leak into the church I lead. Within us resides great beauty and the dynamic capacity to bless others. However, great brokenness also lies within us, holding equal capacity to use our leadership in hurtful ways.[5]

Remissioning churches is a great squeeze. There are moments when the corn disappears the night before you're ready to pick it. Despite the hours and hours of work, emotional labor, and love put into our work, nothing guarantees that things will work out the way you plan or maintain the illusion that you are in control. All your toil doesn't guarantee success. To change your response to the great squeeze, it is helpful to reflect on these questions.

- What is a situation you thought you had under control in your church, only to realize that your best-laid plans were destroyed or dismissed?
- What are some ways you are struggling to connect with God because of the disappointment ministry brings?
- What is one area in your soul that you ignore but find leaking out when you experience a great squeeze?

Moving From Host to Guest

The movement from ownership to stewardship requires a new posture in our relationships. This shift is about learning how to move from host to guest.

When Jesus sends out the seventy-two disciples in Luke 10, he tells them not to take money, supplies, or security. When they reach their destinations, they are to knock on doors and enter where they are invited in, eating what is set before them and enjoying the peace offered to them. They start by identifying people of peace who will invite them into their homes.

A guest in God's work. Why do you feel called to help remission a church? Are you hoping to grow a platform and become a speaker? Are you looking for security? Do you want to be perceived as having it together? Are you hoping for power or control? Do you recognize the immense gift it is to be sent out on mission by God?

The internal shift from host to guest involves relinquishing control and being willing to submit to the bigger mission of God. We are invited guests, receiving incredible hospitality from the Creator of the universe to join in a huge, overarching mission to restore the world to its intended wholeness. But this isn't our brainchild or your idea. We are welcomed, invited, and dearly beloved guests—but we are not in charge of the party. The movement is much greater than any one of our individual leadership efforts.

Stewardship is releasing control, but it is *not* the absence of leadership. Being a guest is a shift in posture rooted in a spirituality of weakness where true leadership looks like service and a willingness to be in a less powerful position.

The gift of leadership. In churches, it can be tempting for pastors to enjoy the position of magical, know-it-all leader. In your next meeting, notice how people defer to your ideas, thoughts, and concerns. Pay attention to their body posture toward you. Pay attention to your own feelings when they defer to your preferences. People can develop unhealthy practices of deferring to leadership even when they disagree, slowly losing touch with their own ability to discern the Spirit and becoming consumers of whatever the pastor or leaders produce.

What does it look like instead to listen to and discern together? How do you as a leader model listening and learning from people in your church? Do you learn from the lessons they have discovered in their vocation? Do you trust that the Spirit can work deeply in them without seminary degrees and they can teach you something you don't know?

This shift from host to guest in the remissioning process means receiving the opportunity to lead, love, and serve the people of your church as a gift instead of a chore. If you spend the bulk of your time complaining about the people God has called you to, it may be a sign of burnout or the need for spiritual direction or counseling.

Learn from the world. As you shift as a leader to receiving the hospitality of the triune God in your everyday life and learn how to lead through submission to others in the church, you need to also learn to be a guest in the world your church is called to serve. When is the last time you were a guest in the home of someone in your community who didn't have anything to do with your church? When is the last time you shared coffee or conversation with someone in your community who does not follow Jesus and learned something from them?

Moving from host to guest in your relationships in the community looks like listening first and speaking second. (Or, better yet, listen first, serve second, and speak third!) How can we truly love our neighbors without getting to know them? Is it any wonder the church proclaims a gospel our community cannot hear because we've not taken the time to learn who our neighbors are and be received as guests in their lives, homes, and world? We've seen the effects of a colonialist expansion of the church and its self-righteous fruit. David Fitch talks about the kind of faithful presence that helps us to live on mission when he highlights that "the disciples go as guests. Don't move from house to house. Instead, be present, submit, eat what is offered, be a guest, put yourself at the mercy of the order and relationships in this place."[6]

Many remissioning leaders find it helpful to serve under the leadership of people in the community. I know pastors who serve on school advisory boards and local nonprofits, join government volunteer positions, help coach sports teams, and find other opportunities where they're not the lead voice. Can you serve when you don't get to call the shots? Will you be the note-taker of the group? Will you help empower women and BIPOC leaders in your community as you sit under their leadership so you might grow more aware of who your neighbors are, learn of their capacity for leadership, share platform space, and grow aware of your own biases and blind spots? How can you lead your church to love your neighbors if you don't know them or serve with them? One of the fastest ways to reduce misunderstandings is to seek proximity and presence in your relationships.

As a remissioning church leader, you help steward your relational capital by spending it serving others.

Remissioning churches have at their center a shift from control to interdependence and humility. The dismantling of Christendom and movement of the church into the margins provides us with new opportunities to recalibrate our existence and live as guests instead of hosts. Look for opportunities to ask questions like:

- What practices help you submit your life to God and be reminded that you are not in control?
- How can you be a guest on a committee/team/leadership meeting this week?
- Who in your community could you learn from this week and practice being their guest?

Here are some action steps you can take to reflect with others about how to be a disciple:

- Start a book group to discuss MacDonald's *Who Stole My Church?* Take time to hear the loss that people in your church feel when they discuss change.
- Invite a community leader you admire to a meal or for a drink so you can learn from them. Offer to pay for the meal/drink, come prepared with questions about their work, and resist the urge to tell your story unless asked.
- Find a spiritual director who can help you develop a spiritual practice to grow in humility in your life with God.
- Find a therapist who can help you to delve beneath the surface of your emotional life and relationships.
- Ask a loved one to share with you something they think would be helpful for you to grow in as a leader.
- Ask for the opinions, insights, and perspectives of others in a meeting before offering your own.

FURTHER READING

Justin Whitmel Earley, *The Common Rule: Habits of Purpose for an Age of Distraction* (Downers Grove, IL: InterVarsity Press, 2019).

Mandy Smith, *The Vulnerable Pastor: How Human Limitations Empower Our Ministry* (Downers Grove, IL: InterVarsity Press, 2015).

Gordon MacDonald, *Who Stole My Church? What to Do When the Church You Love Tries to Enter the 21st Century* (Nashville: Thomas Nelson, 2011).

PART TWO

PRACTICING RESURRECTION THROUGH CREATIVE DESTRUCTION

No one is going to follow you off the map unless they trust you on the map.

TOD BOLSINGER, *CANOEING THE MOUNTAINS*

I call out—
I'm ready, Halmoni!
Come prick my heart
Wrap me with your thread of resilience
I'm bent low
No longer afraid of the needle
More afraid of becoming like stone

GRACE P. CHO, *VOICES OF LAMENT*

5

CREATIVE DESTRUCTION: REMISSIONING FROM DEATH TO LIFE

*In other words, the problem that is usually being visualized
is how capitalism administers existing structures, whereas the
relevant problem is how it creates and destroys them.*

JOSEPH A. SCHUMPETER, CAPITALISM, SOCIALISM, AND DEMOCRACY

*Then Jesus told his disciples, "If any want to become my followers, let them
deny themselves and take up their cross and follow me. For those who want to
save their life will lose it, and those who lose their life for my sake will find it."*

MATTHEW 16:24-25 (NRSV)

ONE OF THE EASIEST WAYS to understand creative destruction is to think about how we've consumed music over the years. In my lifetime I've listened to music on vinyl, cassette, compact disc, MP3, and streaming. Every decade or so music became more mobile, and like other kinds of media, music became owned less and accessed digitally more often. In most instances one form of media was destroyed or fundamentally disrupted by the new form of media. Joseph Schumpeter, who coined the phrase in a book about global markets and change, describes creative destruction as something that is unintentional and happens *to* you. An industry, market, or field of work is destroyed by something new that comes after it.[1]

As you can imagine, vinyl companies weren't excited about cassettes, cassettes about compact discs, and so on. The disruption brought about the death or near death of each of those forms of media. And the death of one form of media led to the birth of another.

It's easy to see this in the story of Kodak, the once-heralded photography company that thrived off its printed work. In 1975, Steve Sasson, a Kodak engineer, developed a digital camera, and the corporate response was to chuckle and put it on a shelf. Kodak was completely disinterested in disrupting its thriving film business. They didn't see how their own creation could lead to the company's demise if they didn't take the innovation seriously.

In early projections Kodak believed it had a ten-year window to prepare for the shift to digital photography and instead focused on improving the quality of its film. Sasson's digital camera patent expired in 2007, and in 2012 Kodak filed for bankruptcy. In life we can lament the changes that come our way and let them happen to us, or we can engage with them and make decisions about what our faithfulness looks like in an ever-changing world.[2]

Creative destruction is an act of dying so something new might emerge.[3] But how do we know what needs to die?

GROWING MEMORIES OF CHANGE

Central to our faith is the life-death-resurrection motif. The big story of Scripture is meant to spark our imaginations, root our lives, and guide our relationships with one another and the world. For far too long, established churches have individualized that narrative and tried to set their aims on constantly growing, adding programs, and chasing success without asking how they are also dying well.

Creative destruction is not an obliteration of the past or an escape to the future. Creative destruction is a hopeful process in which a church leaps into a new era. Churches can observe how this process has occurred in other contexts, such as the formation of the United States. Many elements of the colonists' governance, family life, military, and communication came from British tradition, yet they chose to definitively become a new country. Colonies died and a country was born. The printing press was a new way of communication born from oral storytelling that led to individual experiences with a static text that flattened hierarchical institutions of interpretation.

Like Neil Armstrong said when he stepped on the moon, sometimes what feels like "one small step for a man, [is] one giant leap for mankind."[4] That is, there are times when organizations must take a great leap forward after a series of smaller steps. From believing at one point in history that the sun revolved around the earth to watching a man walking on the moon, humans have done both: taken small evolutionary steps in understanding how the universe was ordered and leapt forward in scientific theory to explore new horizons of possibility. Neil Armstrong's comments on the moon reveal the hope at the heart of creative destruction, which resonates with Paul's exclamation in 2 Corinthians: "So if anyone is in Christ, there is a new creation: everything old has passed away; see, everything has become new!" (2 Cor 5:17 NRSV).

For your church and for followers of Jesus, creative destruction is not mere destruction. It is not the demolition of the old ways of being church with no hope of new life on the other side. It is an intentional process of dying so new ways of being church can emerge. It is a way of intentionally embracing the cross so the new creation can break in. It is a way of living out what we pray in the Lord's Prayer: that God's will be done on earth as it is in heaven.

It may be helpful to reflect on your life and ways you have personally changed over time, as well as changes you have observed in your church or organization:

- What habit or practice in your own life has had to die for you to grow or be healthy?
- What program in your church has gone away, allowing something new to emerge?
- What program in your church requires too many resources without helping you create reproducible disciples?

How Wolves Change Rivers

A fascinating example of creative destruction in nature is shown in a short film about the reintroduction of wolves into Yellowstone National Park after they were absent nearly seventy years.[5] Wolves are hunters, but they also create life for other species. The deer population in Yellowstone had gotten out of control because of the absence of wolves and other predators. Human attempts to control the deer led to the erosion of vegetation and an insignificant decrease in the population. When a small population of wolves was reintroduced into the park, they did hunt and kill some of the deer, but more interestingly, they changed the deer's habits. The deer began to hide in locations less easily tracked by the wolves, and as a result, the vegetation in the park resurged with health. First near the banks of the rivers and then extending outward, the vegetation that had been annihilated by the out-of-control deer population came back to life.

In some places trees quintupled in height in six years. They grew on previously barren hillsides, slowing erosion and regenerating the forest. Birds migrated back to the park. Beavers returned and gave life to the rivers. As the wolves killed coyotes, the population of rabbits and mice increased, which allowed foxes, badgers, hawks, weasels, and many other animals to increase in population as well. With more trees and the slowing of erosion, the bear population increased as there were more berries to eat from the regenerating bushes as well as carrion left by the wolves. Because the wolves changed the deer's habits, in a short number of years the vegetation became increasingly healthy and sustainable in the valleys and gorges along the rivers, restoring what had been destroyed by an out-of-sync ecosystem.

Once the trees and vegetation were given the opportunity to grow, they changed the physical course of the rivers, which experienced less erosion and clearer waters. The introduction of wolves (creativity) into the ecosystem brought about death for some animals (destruction) but in turn brought greater thriving for other animal species, along with the park's vegetation and rivers. Creative destruction made possible a greater flourishing for the entire ecosystem and geographical landscape. Death brought the possibility and reality of new life.[6]

Recently, *The New York Times* reexamined the way this process has been understood in communities near Yellowstone, presenting some startling insights about how creative destruction works over time. Erica Berry writes:

> In reality, the more people live with wolves, the less controversial the animals become. And the inclusive model of community-led conservation spearheaded by Colorado and the Western Landowners Alliance can be applied to other environmental and social issues. The Blackfoot Challenge refers to its consensus-based approach as the 80/20 rule: Focus on finding the 80 percent that participants agree on, then build trust and relationships as you approach the final 20 percent. In our age of polarization, it's a ratio that policymakers and the rest of us should remember. Finding shared values—a sustainable future, say, and safety for our children—is the first step to overcoming disagreement. Every canyon is also an opportunity to build a bridge.[7]

In times of transition, churches and organizations often become overwhelmed at the cost of change. They see every new idea about how to run a program or adjust technology like a wolf hunting prey. What if instead of living in a constant state of worry and avoidance of death, followers of Jesus embraced an active dying so something new could emerge?

In seasons of change, I suggest that churches be purposeful and communicate clearly rather than trying to release wolves secretly into the organization. What if church leaders handed out those cheesy wolf-howling-at-the-moon T-shirts? And when people inevitably ask, "Why are we doing this?" and "Do we need to still do this?" leaders could help their team name what needs to die so a new set of practices could emerge. Instead of creating fear, the wolf pack becomes a funny way to acknowledge that change is hard and sometimes we feel like we're being hunted—but it's also incredibly healthy for the ecosystem at large.

I realize that biblical references to wolves are not usually positive, so the idea of dressing up with wolf T-shirts may feel a bit over the top, but the fact remains that creative destruction helps us hold less tightly to our events, programs, and work so the mission can stay at the center of what we do and why. Wolf pack T-shirts might also help relieve the pressure we feel when we realize someone else's work will not go on forever—just as our own work may have a shelf life too.

RESURRECTION HAPPENS AFTER DEATH

One of the challenges of remissioning an established church is the need to re-narrate our understanding of the good news. Our culture has promised that if we use their toothpaste, obey our thirst, drive their car, sleep on their bed, and have enough money we will find life and life to the full. Churches have believed this too. We can have all the programs. We can have all the partners. We can have all the activities. We can grow and grow, add and add, never being honest with ourselves that it isn't working and we don't have unlimited time or resources.

The long and short of it is this: Our churches won't experience resurrection without death. The invitation to follow Jesus toward the resurrection through the cross is present in each synoptic Gospel. As in baptism, we participate in the cross as individuals within community. Mark 8:34-37 (NRSV) says, "He called the crowd with his disciples, and said to them, 'If any want to become my followers, let them deny themselves and take up their cross and follow me. For those who want to save their life will lose it, and those who lose their life for my sake, and for the sake of the gospel, will save it. For what will it profit them to gain the whole world and forfeit their life? Indeed, what can they give in return for their life?'"

We may be baptized one at a time, but we are not baptized as individuals. Our formation and discipleship take place in community, including the invitation to follow Jesus and take up the cross. When the church is gathered or scattered institutionally, "the church has crosses to take up and on which to suffer for the sake of Christ. The church is an offering, a sacrifice, a Corpus Christi. The church has its own deaths to die Eucharistically."[8] The path of the cross is wide enough for a group of people to travel together, and on that journey we remember whose footsteps we are following, the Christ who both invited us and traveled ahead to show us the way. When discipleship doesn't include the cross but is an escape-from-hell plan, participation in the work of dying to new life seems unnecessary. Discipleship that takes seriously the invitation of the cross avoids the illusion that following Jesus is always easy and fun.

Creative destruction can happen to your church like MP3s treated compact discs, or you can intentionally embrace the cross as a pathway to new life.

GATHER STORIES

Sometimes creative destruction happens to a program or church methodology. For example, established churches often remission their communication practices. One established church used to print a newsletter as its main source of communication and distributed it only in person on Sundays. If you missed worship that week, you missed important announcements, changes to programming, and upcoming events. Eventually the newsletter was replaced by a multipronged communication plan that connected across generations and was specialized to different ministry areas.

Creative destruction can also look like the merger of Mill City Church and Elim Church in Minneapolis.[9] Elim Church was 134 years old, and after long seasons of creative ministry and work in the city, its numerical decline was sped up by the pandemic in 2020. Wanting to still join the mission of God for their neighborhood, the leadership began to explore ways to take up their cross for the sake of their community and sister churches that might benefit from their sacrifice. The merger meant a shift in leadership structure, Mill City moving its campus to Elim Church for worship, discerning which mission pathways to maintain and which to let go, and the death of one congregation by name when it merged with another. This merger was a way to bury and resurrect, marked by extensive communication, clear decision points, and invitation to shared mission. The leaders didn't try to hide the losses or sacrifices each congregation had to make.

By nature, creative destruction is a disruptive process. It is an intentional exploration of what might be left behind so a vision of the future can come into focus. Mill City Church and Elim Church took time to know each other's stories and histories, times when each had navigated change and responded to their evolving communities. A helpful way to learn where creative destruction could be applied in your context is to conduct a series of interviews with people both in your church and in your local community. Deploy the interview chart in table 5.1 with your leadership team, staff, and local leaders to learn how creative destruction has already happened in your community.

Table 5.1. Creative destruction interview chart

Business leader	Longtime church member
• Describe an experience when you realized an existing product was no longer viable.	• When was a time of change or conflict that you believed might close the church? How did the church survive?
• How did you pace the change process from the old to the new?	• What future change do you fear could kill the church?
• What is something you learned that informed change processes for other products?	• What was one of the most successful times of change in the church? What made it go so well?
	• What is something you learned about God through the change process?
Community leader	**Church leader**
• What is a practice that often keeps you stuck in a relational rut?	• Describe a time when a sacred cow was named and buried and the church moved forward together?
• What are ways you are resistant to change in your own life?	• What is a current practice, program, or other area of church that's making it hard for the church to mature and be healthy?
• What is one time you successfully navigated a change that disrupted a relationship or core part of your leadership?	• What would happen if a current sacred cow no longer existed?

One of the reasons people resist change is they easily forget or bury the pain of previous change processes they have already survived. But learning to intentionally reflect on ways your organization has already lived creative destruction can help you inspire the people you lead to remember other challenges they have faced with grace and resiliency. Remissioning asks each of us to consider how our church or organization can choose a collective cross for the sake of a shared new creation.

In my community, a dilapidated gas station was turned into a great barbecue joint within walking distance of my church. Watching how this new business held on to part of the building's history while repurposing the space to meet the growing needs of the neighborhood inspired my leadership team. It caused us to ask questions about where we have blind spots with our own building and campus that can be explored for purposes of creative destruction.

Another church, Old Town Community Church in Alexandria, Virginia, repurposed its building, made its worship space more accessible and communal, and partnered directly with other churches to creatively think about how to live on mission together. OTCC transformed its office and education building to become a hub for local nonprofits. Using a theme of "the common good," they welcomed organizations that empower women through baking, community support and advocacy, counseling services, and more. In a fast-paced commuter culture, OTCC recognized they could disciple people in small groups scattered around Northern Virginia and bury the traditional uses of their building to bless their surrounding community.[10]

What are some ways your church can bury existing programming, outdated methods of communication, no-longer-functioning discipleship pathways, or other assets so you might see new life emerge—not only in your church but in your community?

FURTHER READING

Alan Deutschman, *Change or Die: The Three Keys to Change at Work and in Life* (New York: Harper Business, 2007).

Clayton M. Christensen, *Disrupting Class: How Disruptive Innovation Will Change the Way the World Learns* (New York: McGraw-Hill, 2008).

Seth Godin, "The Race to the Bottom," Seth's Blog, August 20, 2012, https://seths .blog/2012/08/the-race-to-the-bottom.

6

REMISSIONING WITH FRESH EYES

The Word became flesh and blood, and moved into the neighborhood.
JOHN 1:14 (MSG)

Attention is the rarest and purest form of generosity.
SIMONE WEIL, *FIRST AND LAST NOTEBOOKS*

*When institutions fail it is living, breathing human
beings and not mental abstractions that fail.*
HUGH HECLO, *ON THINKING INSTITUTIONALLY*

WHEN I FIRST ARRIVED at the established church I served in Ashland, Virginia, I was struck by the number of signs displayed throughout the building. Some were large, like the six-foot-tall banner in a main thoroughfare showing stock photos of happy people and the word "Connections." Others were maps of the building so tiny you could hardly read them, especially if you were looking for the emergency exit.

But one specific sign especially stuck out to me in my first few weeks. Like many established churches, this one hoped their new pastor would help them connect with the community, reignite a new base of young families, and help kids flow through the halls again. The sign was situated in the main hallway where kids and their families made their way to discipleship spaces, a busy corridor where adults and children navigated past, through, and around each other.

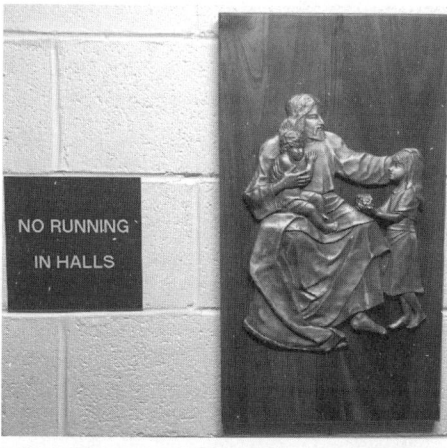

Figure 6.1. No running in halls

With a sign like this, I wonder why families and kids didn't feel welcome at our church? I mean, nothing says Jesus loves the little children like making it clear that Jesus' love is conditional on your speed moving up and down the hallways!

After my first year at the church, I took the leadership committee on a walk down the hallway. At that point we shared enough relational capital that we could have an uncomfortable conversation about how our signs and symbols were impacting our relationships. We stood in front of the bronze Jesus plaque next to "No Running in Halls" and talked about values, hopes, dreams, fears, language, and places. This led to conversations about rituals and practices and the end goal of our discipleship together.

The juxtaposition of Jesus with the little children and the "No Running in Halls" sign is a great insight into what many established churches are struggling to do: they desire new ways of being faithful to the mission of God, but they are embedded in theologies, systems, values, practices, and rituals that suffocate them and diminish their ability to yield fruit consistent with the Spirit for the sake of the world. Dallas Willard's insight from *The Divine Conspiracy* is uncomfortably true: "Your system is perfectly designed to yield the result you are getting."[1] This profound though painful truth must be respected by all who have an interest in Christian spiritual formation, whether for themselves as individuals or for groups or institutions.

I'd like for you to explore the cultural components of your established church. In examining your space, practices, and so on, you'll start to see the gaps between your church's dreams and fears and your culture's dreams and fears, as well as the ways your established church will need to transform to proclaim and live out a gospel your community can understand.

EXEGETING YOUR CHURCH

Similar to the process of exegeting Scripture, it's helpful to examine your church and reflect on the cultural components of your faith community. Table 6.1 is meant to be a guide for learning to see your church.

Table 6.1. Learning to see your church

Established church cultural component	Question	Examples	Implication
Places	Where do people gather, spend time, and relate to one another for formation, community, and relationships?	Homes, church building (and particular spaces in the building, e.g., sanctuary, classrooms), coffee shops	These places serve as part of the church's imagination and as the location for where people gather.
Rituals	What repeatable events, programs, and ceremonies does your church participate in together?	Church seasons, funerals, baby dedications, baptisms, Communion, seasonal activities that have historical or traditional roots	These events or programs give rhythm to how people gather and are born out of history or tradition.
Practices	How does your community come together through worship, formation groups, play, conflict, and mission?	Name specific ways your church practices discipleship, mission, relationships, and worship.	These events or programs give rhythm to how people gather, and they birth new life in the community.
Values	What does your church hold as important, name as being of worth, and lift up as good?	When people are discipled in your context, what does maturity look like?	These values guide the way people relate and support the way you faithfully live into the community.
Dreams	What does your church hope it will become in the years ahead?	Listen to stories people tell when they describe the community flourishing in years to come.	These dreams provide an orientation for what success and flourishing look like to your church.
Fears	What or who does your church fear?	Listen to stories people tell when they describe what they hope will *not* happen in the years to come.	These fears provide an orientation for what failure and disappointment look like to your church.
Language	How does your church communicate with one another and the community?	Digital, social media, apps, print, storefronts, mailings.	This communication tells you about who is in your church.

Next, I recommend the following practical tips to exegete your church. While you can do this exercise by yourself, I recommend inviting someone else (or a group of people) to do this with you. Do you have staff? Deacons? Leadership committees or elders? You don't need to do everything as a group at one time, but ask others to engage with these ideas to gain a broader and deeper perspective as they learn, listen, and imagine with you. It's important to recognize that examining church culture can be intimidating or shame-inducing for some folks. Resist the urge to quickly fix issues you discover. Resist the temptation to soften the conviction the Spirit brings. And do not cast judgment on the people you have been called to serve.

1. Decide to spend significant time in the next few months examining your context.

   - What signs are hanging around your building and what messages do they send?
   - Where do people tend to linger in your church? Why?
   - Are there places where your church gathers and is present in your community?
   - Where are the other intersections between your church and community?

2. Interview people in your church across generations.

   - What are their dreams?
   - What are their fears?
   - What are their dreams and fears for the church and the community?
   - What church communications do they feel hit the mark? What communications confuse them?
   - What rituals and practices give shape to their formation?
   - How can you help them grow in their relationship with Christ?

3. Spend time learning about what really happens in your discipleship spaces.

   - When is the last time you served in the nursery? In a senior adult class? Serve in places you rarely see with people you don't often interact with, even if this means not preaching one week.

- Notice symbols, signs, and markers that communicate values (whether intended or not).
- What do you see and hear when people gather together?

4. Fill out the chart in table 6.1 with a group of leaders.

- What do you learn about your church?
- What are you conveying to others about what it means to be church with you, whether intentionally or unintentionally?
- Whose stories are missing from your church community?
- Go on a prayer walk in your community and ask God to show you the intersections and gaps between your church and community.

Learning to exegete your church is to grow in love for the church and learn how to be with your community as Jesus is with us. Once you learn about your church from the exegesis process, don't leave the information in a binder on a shelf.

- Commit to praying every day for the next month for the eyes to see and ears to hear your church.
- Go on regular prayer walks.
- Ask God to convict you of sin where your church is failing to live up to God's hopes and dreams for your church.
- Ask God to show you where you are being faithful and how to celebrate well.
- Ask God to help you identify the gaps between your church and community and how to begin to build new bridges.

LEARNING TO SEE OUR CULTURE

If we truly want to be on mission, we need to bury the notion that we are bringing God to our community or culture. Churches that think they carry all the "good" and "God" with them can actually do damage in the community when they miss out on the ways God has gone before them in self-giving love.

We see this clearly in Paul's visit to Athens. Paul has been fleeing other communities because of persecution when he finds safe harbor in the city of Athens. As he waits for his team to arrive, he walks around the city. He's overwhelmed by the idols and the disregard for the physical world by the

Epicurean and Stoic philosophers. Paul begins to debate these philosophies with the community and talk about the power of the resurrection. In Acts 17 Paul says:

> People of Athens! I see that in every way you are very religious. For as I walked around and looked carefully at your objects of worship, I even found an altar with this inscription: TO AN UNKNOWN GOD. So you are ignorant of the very thing you worship—and this is what I am going to proclaim to you.
>
> The God who made the world and everything in it is the Lord of heaven and earth and does not live in temples built by human hands. And he is not served by human hands, as if he needed anything. Rather, he himself gives everyone life and breath and everything else. From one man he made all the nations, that they should inhabit the whole earth; and he marked out their appointed times in history and the boundaries of their lands. God did this so that they would seek him and perhaps reach out for him and find him, though he is not far from any one of us. "For in him we live and move and have our being." As some of your own poets have said, "We are his offspring." (Acts 17:22-28)

We see that Paul slowed down, listened, and engaged so deeply in the culture that he could quote their poets, recognize their longing for God, and speak in a way they could hear—because he paid attention first.

One of the biggest challenges established churches face is getting over themselves and the idea that they control where God is at work or that God can work outside their influence and reach. As Acts 17 shows us, the real task is to go where God is already at work!

Paul could see that God was at work because the people were already worshiping gods. They desired to experience and engage in something transcendent. And Paul knew this because he took the time to listen, study, and learn the culture of the city. He knew about the people's worship thoroughly enough that he could reframe their worship of the "unknown God." He knew their philosophers well enough that he could quote them and meaningfully engage in their arguments.

In one of the most startling aspects of this passage, Paul uses the language of the people to name God as "Theos" instead of "Yahweh." He does not force them to assimilate to the Jewish language when naming God in their midst. What are the implications in our context today?

Part of the remissioning process is to recognize that we are not in control and that God's mission does not depend on us or our church. God goes before us. God is stirring up people's hearts and is ahead of us.

These are the guiding principles for what it looks like to be on mission in light of Paul's experience in Athens:

- Enter our neighbors' world.
- Seek the good in what they love.
- Help them find Christ already there.

It can be humbling (some churches would even say humiliating) for established churches to realize that God is at work outside of us. Ahead of us. Sometimes far ahead of us. We must lay that down at the cross. We must confess our blindness and self-centeredness and walk in new life.

To enter our surrounding culture—that is, to be present in our community and seek its flourishing and transformation—we must learn to enter into the worlds of the people in our communities, discover their loves, and help them to name the unknown God who is trying to orient their hearts into God's story of hope. Instead of thinking that we exclusively carry God into culture, how might your church change its posture into one of humility to recognize that it is our work to discover the Spirit already at work?

To enter the world of our neighbors, seek the good in what our neighbors love, and discover Christ already present means that we have to exegete our neighborhoods and learn to live like the kinds of missionaries who know the unknown gods, poets, and philosophers of our day.

Exegeting Our Culture

How much effort has your church put into exegeting your neighborhood? Like Paul in Athens, could your church quote the philosophers and poets of your community? What gods are people worshiping that may be waiting for new names?

How do you understand the culture in which your church is embedded? What are the rhythms, values, patterns, symbols, priorities, and characteristics of the lives of people near you (both geographically and relationally)? To be on mission in your community, you will have to do the time and put in the work culturally for the sake of the good news.

There are at least seven primary components to understanding and exegeting the culture. After reading through table 6.2, take time to make a chart of your own about your own community.

Table 6.2. Learning to see our culture

Cultural Component	Question	Examples	Implication
Places	Where do people gather, spend time, and relate to one another for work, play, and relationships?	Local coffee shops, restaurants, concert venues, bars, parks, historical sites	These places serve as part of the public imagination and as the location for where people gather.
Rituals	What repeatable events, programs, and ceremonies does your community participate in together?	Parades, fairs, special holidays, school functions, seasonal activities that have historical or traditional roots	These events or programs give rhythm to how people gather and are born out of history or tradition.
Practices	How does your community be a community together through work, play, conflict, and relationships?	Parades, fairs, special holidays, school functions, seasonal activities that are future-oriented for who the community desires to become	These events or programs give rhythm to how people gather and are birthing new life in the community.
Values	What does your community hold as important, name as being of worth, and lift up as good?	Freedom, care for the earth, collaboration, innovation, hope, caring, business-friendliness	These values guide the way people relate to and support each other in the community.
Dreams	What does your community hope it will become in the years ahead?	Listen to stories people tell when they describe the community flourishing in the years to come. May include great schools, thriving businesses, great art, being welcoming to new families.	These dreams provide an orientation for what success and flourishing look like in their mind's eye.
Fears	What or who does your community fear?	Listen to the stories people tell when they describe what they hope will *not* happen in the years to come. May include absence of children and young families, closing businesses, struggling schools, lack of diversity	These fears provide an orientation for what failure and disappointment look like in their mind's eye.
Language	How does your community communicate with one another?	Websites, social media, apps, storefronts, bulletin boards, mailings	The communication tells you about the people that live, work, and play in your community.

Following are some practical tips to help you better understand your community. Again, you can engage in this process alone, but I recommend inviting someone else to do it with you.

1. Decide to spend significant time in the months ahead learning from your context.

   - Find places to walk around (especially in nice weather).
   - Find places to linger.
   - Walk after dinner in your neighborhood.
   - Go to a local art show, see a popular movie, or hear a local band.

2. Interview people in your community. Talk to as many people as you can. Ask yourself who the people are who know the community and influence its dreams and fears.

   - School counselors
   - City representatives
   - Longtime faith leaders
   - Coffee shop baristas
   - Longtime business owners
   - Politicians
   - Teachers
   - Historical societies
   - Coaches

3. Before finishing the interview, ask:

   - How can we help?
   - Who else would be helpful for me to talk to?

4. Walk, run, bike, or drive through your community with your eyes, ears, and nose open.

   - Notice statues, symbols, geographical landmarks.
   - Look for dividing lines.

5. Participate in your local community.

   - Show up to town council meetings.

- Be present at parades, parties, community days, and religious holidays for other traditions.
- Hang out at local parks and meet people.
- If your community offers leadership development opportunities, participate.

6. Process with a group of friends or leaders from your church who desire to be present and be good neighbors. You can even make an experience out of it—for example, on second Tuesdays of the month, walk around in your community, share pizza and drinks after, and ask questions like:

- What are we learning about our community?
- What do we see?
- What do we hear?
- What stories are missing?

7. Prayer walk in your community. Learning to exegete a community is to grow in love for the community and learn to be with the community as Jesus is with us. Once you've done the work, don't leave it behind.

- Commit to praying every day for the next month for the eyes to see and ears to hear your neighbors.
- Continue to go on prayer walks.
- Watch some award-winning movies and listen to award-winning music that is outside of your normal genre. Seek to enjoy it with an open posture.

My church took the exegesis of church and culture seriously when we updated our mission, vision, and values. We used outside leadership to encourage us to be honest about our hopes, dreams, and fears, and we intentionally involved feedback from multiple people, organizations, and generations throughout the process—both from inside our church and from the community. Kids from the church designed T-shirts displaying the proposed mission, vision, and values statements to see if they could understand them. We held a community panel asking for our neighbors' perspective on whether the proposed statements were aspirational or currently being practiced by the church. We gained much valuable input by having kids engage with our mission. Community leaders developed new trust for our church, especially local school leaders and nonprofit directors, because they helped shape the language of our heart, hope, and love for our neighbors into language they could understand.

FURTHER READING

Watch the movie *Lady Bird* (directed by Greta Gerwig [New York: A24, 2017]) and pay special attention to the scene between Lady Bird and Sister Sarah Joan focusing on love and attention.

Anne Fadiman, *The Spirit Catches You and You Fall Down: A Hmong Child, Her American Doctors, and the Collision of Two Cultures* (New York: Farrar, Straus and Giroux, 2012 [1997]).

James K. A. Smith, *You Are What You Love: The Spiritual Power of Habit* (Grand Rapids, MI: Brazos, 2016).

Mary Clark Moschella, *Ethnography as a Pastoral Practice: An Introduction,* 2nd ed. (Cleveland, OH: Pilgrim, 2023).

7

PRUNING FOR GROWTH IN THE REMISSIONING GARDEN

There's a different view, and we see it in so many places, but it doesn't get a lot of press, which is the view not based on scarcity but based on abundance. That in an abundance economy, the thing we don't have enough of is enough connection—we're lonely—and we don't have enough time. And if people can offer us connection and meaning and a place where we can be our best selves—yes, we will seek that out.

Seth Godin, "Life, the Internet, and Everything"

One of the great tragedies of the church in America is how many of our most creative leaders poured their energies into creating forms of church life that served just a single generation. . . . Perhaps a new generation of leaders will arise who want to build for posterity, to plant seeds that will take generations to bear fruit, to nurture forms of culture that will be seen as blessings by our children's children.

Andy Crouch, Playing God

For too long churches have been more concerned with surviving than bearing fruit. Long before the pandemic there was a growing sense in established churches that the goal was to simply survive. We have been trying to navigate shifts in technology, how people spend time, generational trends, and expectations for church involvement, among other changes. Somewhere along the line we came to believe it was okay to simply be alive as a church. We didn't *have* to bear fruit. There was no expectation that disciples would be making new disciples. But let's be clear: existence is not the same as bearing fruit.

Pruning branches from a living plant helps it to be more productive and healthy over time. A consistent theme I've heard from church leaders of late is that the pandemic initiated a great pruning that is functioning as an apocalypse. An apocalypse is an unveiling. It reveals what was always true but was previously hidden. The pandemic accelerated a shift that was already underway and has revealed issues that have been impacting our churches for years. This apocalypse unveils who we are. It tells us about the anxieties that lie underneath the surface. It tells us whether we are bent on survival or fruitfulness.

At our home in Ashland, Virginia, we have some knockout rose bushes. I've never had rose bushes before, and during the pandemic, when I had a chance to pay a bit more attention to my yard, I learned some things about these plants. I learned that to prune a rose bush well, there are some things to consider:

- Time: what season is best
- End goal: how large you want the plant to grow; whether you want to plant other rose bushes from the mother plant
- Minor or major pruning: minor pruning happens every year, major pruning every couple of years
- Growing or pruning season: pruning must occur before the plant has produced buds so as not to waste the energy creating those buds

Just as pruning is essential for a rose bush to thrive, pruning is a key part of leading a church.

Zombie Institutions

Churches that are unwilling to repent, prune, and reorient their habits toward the *telos* of the mission of God will die, and their death will not lead to new life.[1] Instead, their death will add to the toxic and ever-present suspicion already present toward churches while casting an even greater shadow of anxiety on organizations around it.

Andy Crouch calls these "zombie institutions," organizations that have emphasized self-preservation over risk and continued learning.[2] He says:

> Zombie churches exist to keep the lights on rather than to be the light in dark places; they turn inward rather than outward; they serve insiders and ignore outsiders.
>
> The paradox of institutional life is very much like the paradox of individual life: only those who are willing to die can truly live. Only institutions that squarely face their own decay and decline can avoid the fate of the zombies.[3]

When churches build their habits, programs, and events around self-preservation, the amount of pruning necessary for growth becomes much greater. Creative destruction isn't merely destruction—it is death for new life. Zombie institutions are the walking dead, people stuck in a traditionalism that no longer makes sense and is devoid of creativity, preventing the future from shaping the present.

So how do we avoid becoming zombie churches? Through pruning, which is a form of creative destruction. As Jesus tells his disciples in the Gospel of John, "I am the true vine, and my Father is the vinegrower. He removes every branch in me that bears no fruit. Every branch that bears fruit he prunes to make it bear more fruit" (Jn 15:1-2 NRSV). Pruning leads to a more excellent life. Pruning can involve the death of programs, transitioning of staff, parishioners leaving, and more. When churches participate in an intentional pruning process—whether the goal is greater social impact, reduction in poverty, enhanced worship culture, or improved education—it becomes possible to bear more fruit. Pruning doesn't guarantee productivity, but it prepares the church ecosystem for the possibility of new life.

Pruning happens when a church intentionally takes up its cross, naming and confessing the brokenness that distracts it from the full scope of God's mission through Jesus for the sake of the world. Creative destruction is the hopeful embrace of the cross to experience the power of the resurrection.

Seth Godin, the branding and marketing guru, describes a turning point in his career that resulted from firing a client who accounted for two-thirds of his company's work. The stress and destruction caused by the client were tearing his company apart, leading to less productivity and a terrible work environment. When firing that client Godin felt an emptiness in the pit of his stomach, because he knew he wouldn't have long to make up the work and keep paying his employees. But the flip side was worse: he didn't want to work with jerks and become the kind of company that was good at working with jerks.[4]

Is your church run or deeply influenced by people who are destroying your future? Are your programs running without clear evaluation of their outcomes? Are the people you are trying to serve being served, or are they being dismissed by religious insiders? Often in our churches there is a high tolerance for simply surviving without bearing fruit, or being content without asking if communal life is shaping us to live like Jesus in the world.

MAKING THE CUT

Very rarely is a church rotten to the core. More often the congregation is distracted, having lost sight of the mission and struggling to recalibrate their work around disciple-making instead of doing things "the way we've always done it."

Pruning means to cut programs, committees, mission projects, and leadership positions not because they are dead, but because they are not bearing (enough) fruit. This may go against our sensibilities, but in John 15 Jesus talks about how even the branches that bear fruit will be pruned so they might bear even more fruit.

It is rare for a church to bear no fruit. But it is less rare for a church to be content with its meager harvest. Some churches choose not to do the pruning necessary for greater fruitfulness. There are four main reasons why this may be:

- It takes too much time to discern what to cut.
- Too many resources would have to shift from church-centric to mission-centric purposes.
- It is too late for pruning.
- There is a desire to avoid conflict.

When you are in survival mode, it is difficult to have the complicated conversations with people about what needs to be cut. It's especially hard when those programs, events, and groups are still functioning. Because pruning is cutting things that are alive and yet unproductive, it can be very difficult to have these conversations. However, the muscles you have grown navigating conflict and growing in honesty about the outcomes of the work are good preparation for harder conversations to come.

When a church has turned inward and lost sight of its mission with its neighbors, it is likely to overresource events, programming, and activities that support the church but don't build bridges in the community, making pruning necessary. What resources could be realigned from church-centric activities to community support and opportunities to live on mission?

Churches tend to feel pressure to prune only when they are stuck in a corner with nowhere to go. But that pruning is often too little and too late. When programs have worn out volunteers, expended funds, taken up space on the calendar, and yielded little to no fruit, there is little energy left for regrowth after pruning.

The most common reason churches avoid pruning is to avoid conflict. You may be wondering how you could possibly prune a mission program at your church—it's done so much good! Lives have been changed! People have been fed! Housing needs have been met! I'll be crucified for even bringing this up! I'm not advocating that you walk around your church with a pair of large garden shears, chopping them in the air and laughing maniacally. Pruning is an act of love for the health, fruitfulness, and longevity of the plant. It's important to take your time to come alongside leaders and teams who have programs, events, and projects they love and love to lead. The goal is to disciple your way through the pruning, not win an argument or exercise power and shut people down.

Pruning is often difficult in churches because what is being cut isn't evil or wrong. I've been to churches that have over twenty different collections happening at the same time all over the building—reading glasses, clothes, food, and so on, all for good causes. No one could possibly say these collection efforts were for something terrible. But no one could name all the partner organizations either. How does your church know where to put its energy and time to further the mission if it is siphoning off resources at every donation bin? When my church reduced its donations to our main missions pathways (food, clothes, and home goods for recently resettled refugees, as well as school partnerships), we saw an increase in total giving, a more unified spirit, and clearer impact with our neighbors.

It is often strange for churches to consider cutting back to bear more fruit. It goes against our sensibilities, in that we usually think doing means bearing more fruit. However, pruning helps the whole plant to grow, become healthy, and bear fruit. What would it look like for you to do some pruning in your church's discipleship garden so that your efforts have a chance to become more effective?

FURTHER READING

Seth Godin, "Unreasonable Clients," Seth's Blog, September 20, 2013, https://seths .blog/2013/09/unreasonable-clients.

Geoff Hamilton, *Organic Gardening: The Classic Guide to Growing Fruit, Flowers, and Vegetables the Natural Way* (New York: DK, 2011).

Seth Godin, "Life, the Internet, and Everything," *On Being,* hosted by Krista Tippett, podcast, January 24, 2013, https://onbeing.org/programs/seth-godin-life-the-internet -and-everything-sep2018.

8

THE NATURE OF CHANGE IN
THE REMISSIONING JOURNEY

*Cultural legacies are powerful forces. They have deep roots and long
lives. They persist, generation after generation, virtually intact, even
as the economic and social and demographic conditions that spawned
them have vanished, and they play such a role in directing attitudes and
behavior that we cannot make sense of our world without them.*

MALCOLM GLADWELL, *OUTLIERS*

A CRITICAL STEP IN THE REMISSIONING JOURNEY is learning to
assess gaps in leadership and organizational processes. A common blind spot
is the number of leaders necessary to run the church. Many established
churches share a common theme: leaders must serve on multiple committees
just to keep things operating. One small church I worked with required every
church member to serve on a minimum of three committees to meet the
requirements of its organizational structure. An overwhelmed system that
has no room to live on mission is a church entering into hospice support.

IDENTIFYING THE GAPS

Identifying the leadership, organizational, and cultural gaps in your
context will help you recalibrate your *telos*—your vision of flourishing,
success, and community in light of God's renewal of all things through

Christ—for the sake of your church and its work in the world. By recognizing gaps in leadership, organizational awareness, and cultural expectations, we can navigate remissioning with greater intentionality and purpose. Instead of lamenting shifts in priorities (sports, music, drama, work, etc.), how might we incarnate our faith in the neighborhood like Christ did with us?

Many churches and leaders are lamenting the diminished number of people returning to church after the Covid-19 pandemic. Why haven't we figured out that instead of pointing our fingers in frustration, we have a new opportunity to close the gap through mission? Why do we take people off the mission field (literally the soccer fields) instead of equipping and sending them to think and creatively live on mission with God?

Part of the problem is a leadership gap. The mission of the church is meant to be shared by all of us. Rooted in the very nature of Christ, each of us has been given gifts in Christ so we may become mature. Paul says in Ephesians:

> So Christ himself gave the apostles, the prophets, the evangelists, the pastors and teachers, to equip his people for works of service, so that the body of Christ may be built up until we all reach unity in the faith and in the knowledge of the Son of God and become mature, attaining to the whole measure of the fullness of Christ. (Eph 4:11-13)

From the very beginning of time God has developed within each of us a base, a home, a wiring, a way of living, being, and leading within the church and for the mission of God.

Eun Strawser points out in *Centering Discipleship*, "Gifts help equip the whole body of Christ to be a full reflection of Christ. Otherwise, our discipleship will be painfully skewed."[1] The church needs all voices present at the table or we will struggle to lead people through the transformation journey.

Let's explore the main focus and maturity markers for each type of leadership role in the "fivefold gifting," or APEST (apostle, prophet, evangelist, shepherd, teacher), model of ministry (table 8.1). I am grateful for Strawser's vision here and add a specific remissioning lens to the roles.[2]

Table 8.1. Fivefold model of ministry

Leadership Role	Main Focus	Maturity Markers
Apostle	Thriving and sustaining: God's invitation to flourish in community	• Creates sustainable supports for growth • Curates vision and follow-through with disciples for the sake of community • Equips and sends leaders • Creates infrastructure to multiply disciples
Prophet	Liberating and reminding: God's invitation to good relationships	• Reminds disciples of God's faithfulness in the past • Describes what faithfulness in the present could look like • Holds church accountable to process matching the desired telos
Evangelist	Welcoming and pursuing: God's invitation to experience good news	• Pursues "not yet" Jesus-followers with incarnational love • Creates an environment of welcome and hospitality • Embodies and proclaims good news • Cuts regulatory tape
Shepherd	Healing and guiding: God's invitation to wholeness and togetherness	• Develops life-giving friendships within the church • Creates room for wholeness and guides healing in relationships • Remembers the ones they have led
Teacher	Learning and expanding: God's invitation to believe and grow	• Helps to make truth accessible • Grows a learning and curious posture in people • Reminds us to hold on to and seek truth in community and hold our beliefs humbly

Which of these leadership roles are present in your church? Which roles are missing? As you might imagine, most established Western churches elevate shepherds and teachers but tend to disregard or expel apostles and prophets. And based on recent data from the Barna Group, 47 percent of millennials believe it is wrong to share your personal beliefs with someone in hopes that they will come to share your faith, which highlights an impending crisis for evangelism.[3]

Most remissioning churches have a long-established leadership gap that has made it difficult to experience the maturity and fullness of God's hopes for them. These are some questions that can help you wrestle with this gap:

- What leadership roles from the fivefold ministry model are missing from your church?
- What leadership types need to decrease so that others might increase?

THE ORGANIZATION GAP

Hugh Heclo describes suspicion toward institutions as a "modern impasse."[4] Here's how he describes the current state of affairs that has led to this institutional pessimism:

> Lies, short-term thinking, self-promotion, denigration of duty, disregard for larger purposes—all these amount to one common syndrome serving to undermine social trust and institutional values. The names of particular persons and organizations fade from our memory, only to be replaced by the next day's news of scandal and shortsighted stupidity.[5]

Millennials have become aware of the temptation by institutions (and churches are no exception!) to co-opt our imaginations for the sake of profit, enlargement of territory, and siloed power. The questions that haunt me are: can churches be concerned about more than self-preservation? And is the best available *telos* for our churches continued existence? The cost of institutional failure is enormous in scope—it involves whole communities of people—yet it is individuals who feel the result. As Heclo points out, "When institutions fail it is living, breathing human beings and not mental abstractions that fail."[6] While the impact of church failure can be vast, failure is always personal, affecting real people in real places in real time. For my peers who are abandoning established churches and institutions of all shapes and sizes, my hope is that creative destruction can become a habit that reinvigorates their desire to participate in institutions once again.

The organization gap is the distance between the church's and leadership's understanding of where a church is in its life cycle. In figure 8.1, remissioning pathways are represented by dotted lines. Intentional disruption can happen during maturity, the plateau of stability, or any of the other phases of the life cycle leading to death, facilitating a return to birth, growth, and maturity. Creative destruction can and must happen throughout the life cycle of a church, like the pruning of a plant to create the possibility of new life. Until creative destruction weaves through the cultural DNA of a church, the *telos* is usually maturity or stability for most churches. It isn't easy to intentionally disrupt an organization seeking maturity to spur learning or growth. But creative destruction not only helps form new discipleship pathways, theologies, and resources, it also creates an ecosystem that fosters rebirth. It is the intentional destruction of certain practices, or even whole institutions, to facilitate new life.

REMISSIONING PATHWAYS

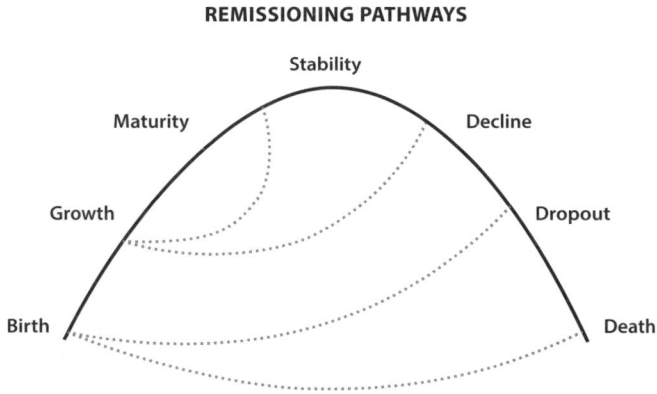

Figure 8.1. Remissioning pathways

Once a church has reached the maturity-stability threshold, it has already begun the march of descent. The further it is along the process toward death, the longer and more radical the destruction must be for the church to experience creativity again.

I've worked with Protestant churches in the UK that are over four hundred years old. Their ceilings have distinct differences depending on which war necessitated their replacement. Some of these churches have remissioned multiple times, changing leadership, denominational affiliation, and mission. One church told me a story about how its people made a significant shift during a season of decline and dropout when the industries around them started to disappear, and the church reflected a similar dispersion. They recognized their struggles and decided to start a ministry for those facing food insecurity. Instead of trying to put all their energy into growing their worship service, they created opportunities for their church to live on mission. They eventually saw a return to worship connected with a clearer way to love their neighbors.

What might it look like for your church to intentionally destroy old habits or forms of being church to create new ones? What might it look like for your church to disrupt its own maturing process to resituate its mission and work in a new context? To decrease the severity of the destructive process, start the disruption earlier so there are fewer sweeping changes necessary.

The main question is: where is your church on the organizational life cycle chart? Or perhaps there are two main questions:

- Where do you think your church is?
- Where does your church think it is?

First, identify where you are on the bell curve, then take some time to choose which dotted line you must travel along to return to the growing and healthy side of the curve. Be honest about where your church is and also about where your church believes it is on the life cycle too. In later chapters we will discuss what those movements from death to life entail in the creative destruction process.

The Nature of Change

It can feel overwhelming at times to consider the way change takes place in our churches. Some folks get angry. Others grow sad. Some become suspicious. Others appear paralyzed.

The challenge for most remissioners is to learn how to regulate their own emotional temperature, to listen, and to read the people in the congregation according to their emotional symptoms rather than the leader's. When people are angry, it isn't fair to assume that they hate the change or that they will not go forward with you. Good leaders will learn to understand the nature of change: it produces varied emotional responses and behaviors that act as signposts revealing where people are in the process.

Remissioning leaders must learn to see emotional and behavioral response as an indicator of movement through the change process—not a refusal to change.

It is tempting to see fear, resentment, resistance, and anxious behavior as signs to turn around in the change process. However, these indicators help you know when and how to press in with both individual and communal change. Ron Heifetz and Marty Linsky help to frame the feelings of loss that come with leading through the remissioning process:

Asking people to leave behind something they have lived with for years or for generations practically invites them to get rid of you. Sometimes leaders are taken out simply because they do not appreciate the sacrifice they are asking from others. To them, the change does not seem like much of a sacrifice, so they have difficulty imagining that it seems that way to others. Yet the status quo may not look so terrible to those immersed in it, and may look pretty good when compared to a future that is unknown. Exercising leadership involves helping organizations and communities figure out what, and whom, they are willing to let go. Of all the values honored by the community, which of them can be sacrificed in the interest of progress?

People are willing to make sacrifices if they see the reason why.[7]

Remembering that it is often the loss people fear and not the change itself can help remissioning leaders hold a posture of empathy rather than anger to what is often experienced as resistance. You would (or should!) not tell a grieving parent to "get over it," so resist the temptation to lose your cool with your people when they are emotionally dysregulated by their sense of loss.

THE REMISSIONING CHANGE CYCLE

One of the things I've learned through working with remissioning churches is that change often operates on a normal, natural, and predictable pattern. This change cycle is helpful in thinking about churches, but it also informs marriage coaching, grief counseling, and other support that I offer my congregants and neighbors. Change doesn't discriminate between its recipients.

The change cycle guide helps you understand where people are on the journey so you can more accurately disciple them into the next stage. If you can help people name their feelings or if you can identify the nature of their behavior, you can discern more clearly what shepherding should look like for them. Change can become less personal and more predictable with the use of this guide, shown in figure 8.2.

Change. The remissioning change cycle begins with a disruption being introduced into the system. It could be a new style of worship, a leadership restructuring, a staff retirement, a moral failure, a large financial gift, and so on. The change could be something good or something bad. The common thread is that it is something new and disruptive to the status quo.

REMISSIONING CHANGE CYCLE

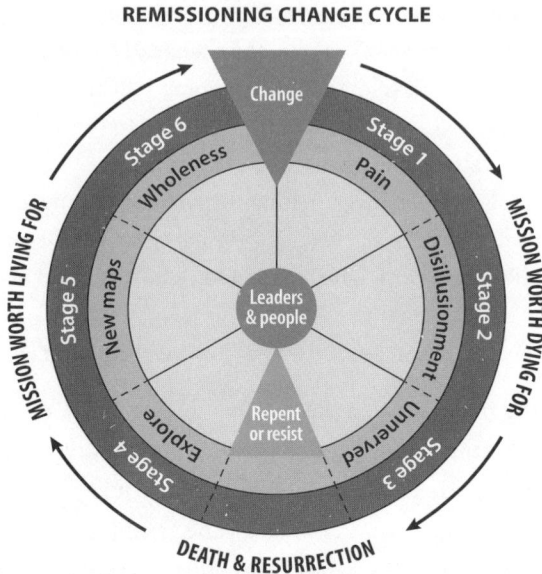

Figure 8.2. Remissioning change cycle

Stage 1: Pain. In this stage, people have feelings like loss, fear, anger, dread, shame, defensiveness, and overwhelming vulnerability. They will have thoughts of suspicion, sadness, worry about who will be left behind, nostalgia, and despair. Their behavior could look like lashing out, angry emails, gossip, immobility, or an unwillingness to try. This initial stage is full of pain because those closest to the change are experiencing the most loss.

Stage 2: Disillusionment. In this stage, people have feelings like apprehension, doubt, anxiety, PTSD, shock, resentment, comparative suffering, pride, and disorientation. This often leads to skepticism, a feeling that leadership is not up to the task, bittersweet memories of loss and possibility, cognitive dissonance, and doubt about the whole remissioning project. You will see behaviors like sabotage, active working against the change, a growing desire for a "back-to-Egypt committee."

Stage 3: Unnerved. In this stage, people often feel unsettled, anxious, unsure, stressed, unsteady, lonely, disconnected, and insecure. These feelings can lead to confusion, scattered thoughts, inability to make clear plans, hesitancy, and inconsistent vision for what's next. The behavior in this stage will look like relational distance in case things don't work out, inefficiency, decreased productivity, sluggishness, anxiety about each step, and a need to work out each piece of the puzzle before taking any action.

The overarching question that is shaping the first three stages is: *Do we have a mission worth dying for?* This part of the journey is cruciform and difficult. Most leaders themselves will lose nerve in stages two and three and turn back before the breakthrough into new life. But God's grace is such that we often get to experience a number of small changes that serve as a kind of workout to grow our adaptive change muscles until our church gets to the "repent-or-resist" point of the cycle. This is the culmination of the wilderness journey before entering the promised land. You either go back to Egypt or you trust God to see you into a new place.

Repent or resist. This part of the change cycle is the threshold from death to life. It is the place where the community and leaders recognize, name, and repent of their complicity in getting stuck, losing sight of God's mission, and loving themselves more than their neighbors. The only way through this part of the change process is to repent. This means the leader and the people specifically name how the change has served as an apocalypse (unveiling and revealing) of the sin or dysfunction that has kept the church from actively living out the two great commands: to love God and love neighbor. This is the cross moment. You may have to wait longer than three days for resurrection, but this is the moment or season when the leaders and church decide together to die to self and be reborn or pine for the leeks in Egypt. It is also possible, with reflection and objective guidance, for the leader to realize he or she holds some responsibility for not adequately discipling the people through the process of navigating loss and change.

If the leaders and church are able, willing, and humble enough to choose acceptance of the change and death to self, a new set of possibilities opens up and the overarching question shifts to: *Do we have a mission worth living for?* This question is rooted in asking what should be rebuilt and created on the other side of loss.

Stage 4: Explore. In this stage people will often feel free, hopeful, trusting, excited; they may have a sense of accomplishment and ease. This leads to thoughts of adventure, new opportunities, plans to try new things, bringing people with us, and sadness for those who are left behind. The behavior in this stage will look like trying and failing without judgment, movement from shame to freedom, people on the sidelines deciding to join in the new work, and new experiments. This stage will feel unproductive but without resentment or anger.

Stage 5: New maps. In this stage people will feel joyful, reflective, calm, non-anxious, wonder-struck, interested, and accomplished. These feelings will lead to thoughts of relief, focus, reverence for the process, and how to move the change into sustainable practice. This will lead to actions like reflective learning with the intention to create sustainability, cultivating and documenting wisdom, asking new questions from the new maps being created, and humble sharing of wisdom. This stage is when the change moves into the center of the work and relationships, and a new way of seeing, living, and relating emerges.

Stage 6: Wholeness. In this stage people will feel trusting, restored, hopeful, and like they are living with integrity in the spiritual and relational aspects of life. This will create thoughts of clarity, unencumbered relationships, courage for other change processes, and resilience, leading to behaviors like empowering others, generosity with resources, belonging to one another, love, trust, and compassion. In this stage, if churches and leaders can seek wholeness, they will learn to navigate change with the whole person in mind and take the actions, feelings, and behaviors of others in change processes less personally.

A church in the Midwest that used the remissioning pathways tool identified itself as careening past the dropout stage into death. A new pastor with a knack for seeing the best in people and honoring the culture of the church and the neighborhood, along with a leadership team desperate enough to change, went on a journey together that started with thinking they would have to close their doors. Instead they are experiencing a restart that has rejuvenated the church and surrounding community. Both the church and pastor surprised themselves by willingly repenting of the ways they had put their own needs before the needs of the community, and they started to clarify how they could make disciples and further their food access work for the sake of their neighborhood.

MAPPING PEOPLE IN THE CHANGE CYCLE

Edwin Friedman helps us see that understanding the change process removes from us the illusion that change can simply be willed through effort. Change requires presence and proximity. He writes:

> Most crises cannot by their very nature be resolved (that is, fixed); they must simply be managed until they work their way through. This is generally a process that cannot be willed, any more than one can make a bean grow by pulling on it. This, of course, puts a premium on self-regulation and the management of anxiety instead of frantically seeking the right solution.[8]

Change is a *process* that has the potential to yield an outcome, but the process itself informs the outcome, or what Friedman calls the "solution." Faithful presence through the process is what helps yield a meaningful outcome. And the process itself is an end—not simply a means to an end.

Try a reflective exercise in which you name a change that has been introduced in your church. Walk through the change cycle guide and identify people in each stage, then describe what presence looks like to those people. Next, describe what discipling people into the next stage looks like through your leadership. It's important to recognize that the process is not a linear progression; people may move forward and then backward and forward again, or simply remain stuck in a stage. The "repent-or-resist" step is a wall many people simply never make it past when navigating change.

I know of a church in a rural community that has had three pastors in six years. Each time a new pastor has gotten close to making their first significant change, usually after a full year of service, the same two leaders have raised a critical voice and disagreed with the change. Whether it was to introduce new songs into worship, adjust the leadership structure, prune the total number of committees, or right-size the budget for the size of the congregation, when the church approached "repent or resist," they chose to resist every time. An interim pastor reached out to me for guidance on how to find breakthrough, and using this chart the pastor was able to invite those leaders to consider letting a major change go through or risk a perpetual merry-go-round of pastors until no one would accept the job.

Many, *many* established churches never make it through stage three into repent-or-resist and out the other side into stage four because the anxiety of the leader becomes too much, the cost seems too high, and the resistance becomes overwhelming. If you knew that the resistance, anxiety, and stress being expressed to/at you was normal and natural, might you be able to differentiate people's behavior from the quality and character of your leadership? Basically, can this chart help you stop taking things so personally when you are navigating change in your church? Let's make it clear: learning to take things less personally and practicing presence with people in change processes is essential in remissioning an established church.

During the pandemic, this chart proved helpful in discerning how to lead through the shutdown, develop and plan regathering phases, chart communication, name challenges in relationships, and clarify differences of opinion on how to go forward together. This chart helped me assess the loss, doubt, and discomfort people were feeling as the isolation and fear of that cultural moment took root in our community. Fear of the "other" took precedence in some people's hearts. Skepticism and political tropes were spelled out in protest, and a general feeling of anxiety boiled over into multiple stages.

The church could have dug in and refused to change, as it had many times before when faced with cultural change. Yet the leaders who held this cycle up as a lens for interpretation helped us, through their proximity and presence, move forward to a decision point about regathering and figure out ways to pace the change.

Leading Through the Remissioning Change Cycle

Learning to lead (think APEST here, not simply shepherding) through change cycles without taking things personally as you more generously assess where people are in the process is a muscle you can develop over time. There are a few critical skills you can practice along the journey to navigate the Mount Everest experiences that will require more of you.

Self-regulation. Navigating change requires learning to regulate your own emotional, relational, and spiritual climate. This means developing a trusted network of relationships with people who are also learning to self-regulate. Sharing language, assessment, and practices together can help you navigate your own experience of the change and handle the heat that comes with being in leadership. What do your daily rhythms and habits look like as the heat gets turned up and you get closer to the danger zone? How do you navigate your anxiety when you make it through the danger zone and you let your foot off the gas a bit? Finding a spiritual director or counselor will be critical, as will intentional friendships. Sharing your experience with a trusted network is critical in discipling people toward a healthier movement in the breadth of the church.

Practicing presence. It can be tempting to avoid people who are full of fear, who express resistance, or who leak their anxiety onto you. Yet being present and in proximity to people in these early stages of change will help you disciple them into learning that change is natural, normal, and predictable. Leaders can unintentionally communicate that "if you aren't with me, you're against me" when we don't practice presence in the midst of change. This doesn't mean we take abuse or give people limitless presence (especially if they are toxic and destructive). Presence also can happen in groups, and remember that Jesus sent the disciples out in pairs. Practicing presence isn't meant to be a solo endeavor. Practicing presence also means proximity and assessment on the other side of the repent-or-resist zone as we build relationships in the new promised land.

Enter the repent-or-resist zone. Often we avoid this zone. We know there are risks, we sense the struggle, and we recognize there may be no turning back if we decide to move into repent or resist. So we avoid the danger and aid in keeping our churches stuck. Not every repent-or-resist experience will be about whether you stay or are fired. (Though the deepest remissioning projects often come to this at some point.) To avoid this zone is to miss the cross and avoid the likelihood of resurrection.

Expect sabotage. If you can remember to expect sabotage as a normal, natural, and predictable part of change, you will be able to assess more accurately where you are in the process. Sabotage is a sign you are getting closer to the point of no return in the repent-or-resist zone (or you are already in it!) and the turn to stages four through six is on the horizon. Sabotage is a sign that the clash of cultural values is being productive and people are having to make personal decisions about how to live into the change. Friedman writes:

> To succeed at a new venture requires a kind of relentless drive that sometimes may seem to border on the demonic. But no one has ever gone from slavery to freedom with the slaveholders cheering them on, nor contributed

significantly to the evolution of our species by working a forty-hour week, nor achieved any significant accomplishment by taking refuge in cynicism.[9]

Sabotage is not a sign of failure but rather that you are getting to the good stuff. The new way is beginning to emerge and the resistance to change points toward the possibility of new life.

Differentiate experiences. Remember that while communally your church may be at one stage in the collective process, individuals are often scattered throughout. Resist pressuring individuals to be where "everyone else is." Instead, with a mix of both invitation and challenge, guide people to name their feelings, identify their thoughts, and reflect on their behavior as a means of discipleship. As you develop more leaders who can navigate relationships using the change cycle chart, you can more intentionally disciple people to embrace the cross and resurrection as they navigate change.

Avoid the quick fix. People may have taken many years to be discipled by their leaders, churches, habits, families, friends, and so on to get to this point in their journey. Avoid the temptation to believe that a quick fix will make everything better. A great sermon might spark an idea, a light-bulb moment, and a person may want to begin to change, but without the necessary habits and community, the change may remain an idea and not become reality. One Bible study, one worship service, one conversation, one song—the quick fix is not how sustainable change takes place. The process itself (navigating the stages) is what develops the muscles to run the race. Remind yourself and other leaders to avoid this temptation as you help people navigate the stages of change and work toward meaningful integration.

On a trip to a conference with several of my leaders to help map out potential changes in worship, we were walking through the airport together when I saw the remissioning change cycle come to life. In our group one leader was far ahead of everyone else. Sometimes this leader looked back across the airport to see if we were still following. A couple people were a good distance away from both the head person and from the middle group. The bulk of the group was in the middle. A couple came behind the middle group, and then one was the furthest behind, bringing up the rear. One of the challenges of remissioning leadership is to recognize that not everyone is at the same place in the change cycle at the same time. However, using the change cycle can help you assess where they are on the journey so you can shepherd them through the process and bring the group along together, even if they are at different stages.

In my church, when we are navigating a significant change, our staff and leadership map people out so we can be more intentional in how we guide, care for, and invite them to take the next step on the remissioning journey with us. When it has been clear through conversations, meetings, and trainings that at least 70 percent of the church is ready to enter the death and resurrection stage, we purposefully name this moment, help people get their bearings, and invite them to decide how to proceed together.

Change isn't easy. Leadership isn't easy. Remissioning a church takes incredible courage and faith that God is still inviting people into the story of the death and resurrection. But when we learn to see the change cycle as part of the normal, natural, and predictable pathway to appropriate disruption and innovation, our emotions find their proper place and we can focus on intentionally discipling our people into healthy patterns of relationship.

FURTHER READING

Roger Martin, *The Opposable Mind: How Successful Leaders Win Through Integrative Thinking* (Cambridge, MA: Harvard Business Review Press, 2007).

Ronald Heifetz and Marty Linsky, *Leadership on the Line: Staying Alive Through the Dangers of Change*, rev. ed. (Cambridge, MA: Harvard Business Review Press, 2017).

Henri Nouwen, *In the Name of Jesus: Reflections on Christian Leadership* (Chestnut Ridge, PA: Crossroad, 1989).

Leroy Barber, *Embrace: God's Radical Shalom for a Divided World* (Downers Grove, IL: InterVarsity Press, 2016).

TRADITIONED INNOVATION

Culture formation is generational, not birthed in a night. Generative thinking can inspire us to work within a vision for culture that is expressed in centuries and millennia rather than quarters, seasons, or fashions. People in the arts work in conversation with artists of the past as they are preparing the future, attempting work with enduring qualities that might in turn speak to new generations.

MAKOTO FUJIMURA, *CULTURE CARE*

If we will embody mutuality, marked by a true understanding that we need one another, we will flourish. If we are openhanded and share power, we will thrive. If we say "yes" to this movement of God, it will simultaneously feel like loss and gain. Will we choose to surrender our power, our preferences, our positions, and receive the gift of renewal?

LISA RODRIGUEZ-WATSON, *RED SKIES*

PART THREE

PRACTICE AND INNOVATION

9

REMISSIONING STARTS WITH THE END

There are no "private" practices; rather practices are social products that come to have an institutional base and expression. Practices don't float in society; rather they find expression and articulation in concrete sites and institutions—which is also how and why they actually shape embodied persons. There are no practices without institutions. Second, a telos *is always already embedded in these practices and institutions. That is, there is an intimate and inextricable link between the* telos *to which we are being oriented and the practices that are shaping us in that direction. The practices "carry" the* telos *in them.*

JAMES K. A. SMITH, *DESIRING THE KINGDOM*

THE GOAL OF REMISSIONING IS NOT CHANGE. The goal or hope of remissioning is new life through transformation. The hope is that our churches will practice shared life together in such a way that the reign of God will transform our brokenness into a place of healing. And our churches become living signposts of what life with God forever will be like one day.

Remissioning churches are people gathered to develop new habits, imaginations, and relationships that transform us from the inside out. In this section, we will explore how our imagined future, remembered past, and burial processes help us to be more intentional with our everyday habits to become churches more closely resembling the fullness of the kingdom of God.

Along with creative destruction we'll explore a new theme of remissioning called "traditioned innovation." Greg Jones describes traditioned innovation here:

> In our thinking as well as our living, we are oriented toward our end, our *telos*: bearing witness to the reign of God. That is what compels innovation. But our end is also our beginning, because we are called to bear witness to the redemptive work of Christ who is the Word that created the world. We are the carriers of that which has gone before us so we can bear witness faithfully to the future.[1]

Traditioned innovation is a way of learning from our past or receiving it in such a way that we can faithfully go in new directions in a manner consistent with the story we have inherited.

OUR HABITS SHAPE OUR LOVE

If someone were to sit in a balcony as your faith community worshiped, observe as you gathered to pray and be on mission, or sit at a table in your favorite restaurant, watch footage from a recent board meeting, and see your production team at work, what would they see?[2] James K. A. Smith wants you to notice the habits and practices of your church that you do instinctually, almost without thinking, as a way to learn about how those habits inform the *telos* of your organization.

In one established church, I noticed that when we said the Lord's Prayer together in worship, the words were nowhere to be found. They weren't in the bulletin, on a screen, in a book, or on a card in front of them in the pew. While saying the prayer was a good thing, an important element in the way we practiced together wasn't being considered, namely: if you were a guest who didn't know the words to the prayer or a child who hadn't learned them yet, you had no way to pray the Lord's Prayer with the church during the service. You were on the outside looking in, even while sitting in the building.[3]

To understand the *telos* of an institution is to look at the kind of people it produces. Or simply put: what kind of disciples is your church making?

The quote from Smith at the start of our chapter is important: there are no private practices. Our shared habits as a church give expression and voice to what we hope for, what we lament, and what we ignore. There is an incredible link between the habits (informed by what we called rituals, practices, language, and places in our cultural exegesis charts) and the vision of flourishing and God's rule and reign being fulfilled.

No habit or practice is contextless or neutral, which isn't to say every habit is equal or holds the same culture-shaping weight. But all habits and practices train our desires toward a certain end.[4] To read the *telos* of a church's habits, we must ask good questions:

> What vision of human flourishing is implicit in this or that practice? What does the good life look like as embedded in cultural rituals? What sort of person will I become after being immersed in this or that cultural liturgy? This is a process that we can describe as cultural exegesis.[5]

Everything we do shapes what we love. And our commitments as a church tell those around us more than we may care to admit. While we might express a commitment to justice and freedom for the oppressed, our shopping habits, political involvement, and faith practices might tell a different story. Our shopping habits may tell a story about new slaves in factories in a distant land who help us buy affordable jeans. Our political habits may emphasize an allegiance to our own nation-state over and against all others. And our faith practices may welcome people who are already on the inside, but to those new to the church there is no invitation into the life of the community or adequate training to acclimate to the particular language game. Without examining our habits, we fail to exegete the trajectory of those habits both individually and institutionally. Worse, we can examine our habits and convince ourselves we have done all we could and be just as invincible of sinners as before.

NAMING OUR *TELOS*

Telos is a Greek word that has to do with our understanding of how things end. As followers of Jesus we have a vision of how God's rule and reign will come into its fullness at the culmination of time, and that shapes our *telos*. Our discipleship pathways, mission pathways, friendships, vocation, parenting, soccer team, and everything else we do has a *telos*—a purpose.

Churches are always more than the sum of their individual parts. Churches are part memory, part presence, and part imagination, but they are also more than each of those three practices of seeing the world. Churches are living and breathing organisms made up of people. People have histories and futures and are trying to figure out how to live in the present. Churches have hearts because they are made of people with shared habits, desires, stories, arguments, and imagination for what it means to be in the world. Those habits, desires, and imaginations are oriented toward an end, a *telos*, that reveals the deepest ordering of love in a particular direction along a particular trajectory. For Christians, the hope for all institutions—not just our churches—is the restoration and reconciliation of all things through the life, death, and resurrection of Christ.[6] Passages like this from Paul's letter to the Colossians help orient our sense of where things are headed:

> He is the image of the invisible God, the firstborn of all creation; for in him all things in heaven and on earth were created, things visible and invisible, whether thrones or dominions or rulers or powers—all things have been created through him and for him. He himself is before all things, and in him all things hold together. He is the head of the body, the church; he is the beginning, the firstborn from the dead, so that he might come to have first place in everything. For in him all the fullness of God was pleased to dwell, and through him God was pleased to reconcile to himself all things, whether on earth or in heaven, by making peace through the blood of his cross. (Col 1:15-20 NRSV)

Or consider this image from Revelation 21 where Jesus has moved into the neighborhood once again:

> Then I saw "a new heaven and a new earth," for the first heaven and the first earth had passed away, and there was no longer any sea. I saw the Holy City, the new Jerusalem, coming down out of heaven from God, prepared as a bride beautifully dressed for her husband. And I heard a loud voice from the throne saying, "Look! God's dwelling place is now among the people, and he will dwell with them. They will be his people, and God himself will be with them and be their God. 'He will wipe every tear from their eyes. There will be no more death' or mourning or crying or pain, for the old order of things has passed away." He who was seated on the throne said, "I am making everything new!" (Rev 21:1-5)

Table 9.1 shows the *telos* of creation as described in these passages.

Table 9.1. *Telos* of creation

Signs of new creation	Examples
Rulers and powers oriented toward healing	Leaders yield power for the sake of better relationships.
Reconciliation of relationships	Broken relationships become whole in families and friendships and between enemies.
Clear sense of God's presence	People sense that God is close and the Spirit is at work.
Physical healing	Our bodies are being restored and made whole.
New life out of death	Out of brokenness, pain, and even death new ways of being church and neighbor emerge.

What stories give orientation to your church's *telos*? Are there passages of Scripture, stories of the future, hopes and dreams that provide horizons for your faith community to work toward together? To bring this closer to home, is your vision of the rule and reign of God more than a successful Sunday morning worship experience?

UP, IN, AND OUT TOGETHER

Many established churches have a vision of flourishing and *telos* that is too narrow or shortsighted. Often the vision is focused on a great preacher, meaningful and passionate worship, and strong programs with a few events scattered in along the way. But if the vision of flourishing is the reconciliation of people with God, the healing of creation, and God's presence fully with us, might there be a vision of success that includes our neighborhoods, relationships, and churches in a more robust way?

In chapter two we looked at the importance of a leader having a rhythm of life that involves movement upward with God, inward with the church, and outward with neighbors. Let's look at this pattern again (see figure 9.1) to explore how our churches create a communal rhythm of life together.

The aim of "up" is communion and meaningful relationship with God; it is living into the vision that God desires to dwell with us and we may enjoy our lives in proximity

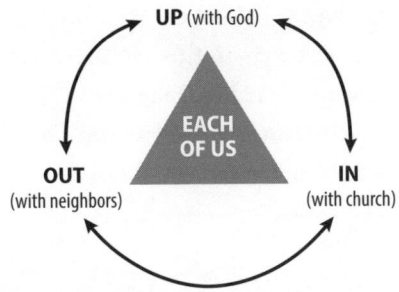

Figure 9.1. The remissioning discipleship triangle

and relationship with him. As Revelation 21:1-5 reflects, we are with God and God is with us and we dwell in close relationship together. This is about much more than meeting for worship or prayer gatherings once a month. It is about living with God in our everyday life, communing with him as he communes with us.

The aim of "in" is living as God's family together. In Acts we see the church eating together, working together, praying together, and living as family regardless of the biological families they came from. Church is about living in deep relationship with one another, sharing not only the religious aspects of our lives in surface encounters, but seeing each other for who we really are and abiding deeply in relationship.

The aim of "out" is to understand that we are the body of Christ, gifted and empowered by the Spirt to seek the renewal of all things. We are co-missioned to live out the hopes and dreams of Christ on earth as in heaven, proclaiming and living the good news for all people. We are foretastes and instruments of the coming reign of God in the here and now. And we chase after God's presence in the neighborhoods, cities, fields, and communities where we share life with our neighbors.

A church that lives out these three integral ways of being—up, in, and out—will see that each aspect informs the other and helps relationships to deepen, healing to take place, and the mission of God to be lived out in the world. We must consider how in between our times of communal gathering we extend the up, in, and out in our daily lives as leaders and in the disciples we are making. When we are scattered throughout the week, how are we living out our shared faith in the world?

With your team, examine how your church is living up, in, and out in everyday life. What signs of the new creation do you need to spend more time living into in this season of your life as a church? Let's reexamine the remissioning rule of life from chapter four but this time think about the way your church organizes its time, programs, events, gathered and scattered practices, and mission.

Table 9.2. Up, out, and in rule of life

Up with God	
Worship	
Study	
Prayer	
Art	

In with church	Out with neighbors
Discipleship groups	Serving together
Meetups	Meetups
Caring for one another	Joining in activities of neighbors
Navigating conflict	Caring for one another

Here are some insights to help you with this exercise. Remember, while you can do it on your own, there's a lot to be gained by engaging a leadership team or staff to join you.

- First, take time to sketch out the already existing programs, events, meetups, discipleship groups, and so on in both your gathered and scattered rhythms as a church. Then, describe what these rhythms would look like in an ideal situation.
- Reflect back on your remissioning exegesis charts from chapter six. What is missing from your shared rule of life? What needs pruning?
- What do you need to make sure to hold on to as you remission?
- What groups of people are not currently included?
- Can you map out a calendar based on the rule and rhythm of life you created? What is the pacing? Is there room for people to live "out" with neighbors?
- How can an examination of your present inform a clearer articulation of a *telos*?

One midsized Protestant church created a communal rhythm of life based on the surrounding farming community in conjunction with the school year. When planting occurred in late summer and the start of fall and as the school year began, the church invited members, friends, and neighbors to start fresh together. They presented new opportunities to enter discipleship groups, serve in the food pantry, and connect in worship. Heading into winter they eased their programs' pace but accentuated care, one-time events (meetups), and discipleship groups to help people grow while recognizing that the cold weather often diminished people's energy levels. As spring came into view, they fertilized the ground with fresh activities and service opportunities, then invited people to take a new step to mature in their faith. The summer became a time of rest as people scattered on vacations, which gave groups, leaders, and people a chance to recharge.

A practical way my own church lives out this chart is to give simple instructions for the rhythm of our discipleship groups. Each month we ask them to meet twice to connect up with God, once with each other to grow in relationship, and once living on mission together. We remind our leaders that they don't have to create all of the opportunities to live in and out together. They can join scheduled activities happening in the community, like Fourth Fridays, which feature live music and food trucks in our downtown. They can simply meet up there as a group or invite friends to join to build relationships with neighbors. We also create a discipleship guide each week with an "up, in, and out" framework for groups to connect faith and activities to the Scriptures.

THE PAST GETS IN OUR EYES

In the old comic *Peanuts*, Charlie Brown and Lucy are on a baseball team together. For a few seasons now their team hasn't won a game. But a new season has begun and there is hope—the kind of hope that is possible only when no pitch has been thrown and no one has gotten up to bat.

Charlie Brown is the pitcher, and as he throws the ball toward home plate the batter smacks it into the outfield, where Lucy is ready to catch the high fly ball. Lucy watches, waits, extends her arm, reaches for the ball—and misses. The ball falls past her glove to the ground. When she brings it back to Charlie Brown to apologize for missing the easy catch, Lucy says, "I thought I had it, but suddenly I remembered all the others I've missed. The past got in my eyes!"

Does this sound familiar to you as you lead your church? "The past got in my eyes!" One of the primary reasons we must be so intentional in naming the ways we gather, scatter, commune, and relate to each other, God, and neighbors is that the past often makes it difficult to see the present and the future. We can also develop habits that blind us to the new life God has for us. Sometimes is it our successes and other times our failures that keep us from moving into faithful expressions of our faith for today while remaining faithfully connected to our tradition.

Lucy may be right: the past gets in our eyes. Yet when a church intentionally thinks about its communal rule of life together, it can hold the creative tension of growing closer to God, each another, and its neighbors and learn to catch whatever fly ball comes its way.

Further Reading

L. Gregory Jones, "Traditioned Innovation," Faith & Leadership, Duke Divinity School, January 19, 2009, https://faithandleadership.com/traditioned-innovation-0.

Greg Jones and C. Kavin Rowe, *Thriving Communities: The Pattern of Church Life Then and Now* (Durham, NC: Faith & Leadership, 2014).

James K. A. Smith, *Desiring the Kingdom: Worship, Worldview, and Cultural Formation* (Grand Rapids, MI: Baker Academic, 2009).

James K. A. Smith, *Imagining the Kingdom: How Worship Works* (Grand Rapids: MI: Baker Academic, 2013).

Natasha Sistrunk Robinson, ed. *Voices of Lament: Reflections on Brokenness and Hope in a World Longing for Justice* (Grand Rapids, MI: Revell, 2022).

Joshua Hayden, *Sacred Hope,* Ancient Faith Series (Kansas City, MO: Foundry Publishing, 2010).

N. T. Wright, *Surprised by Hope: Rethinking Heaven, the Resurrection, and the Mission of the Church* (New York: HarperOne, 2008).

10

REMISSIONING AND THE
WORK OF REMEMBERING

Remember that you were slaves in Egypt
and the LORD your God redeemed you.

DEUTERONOMY 15:15

By your stabilizing hand, you keep our heads raised
and our eyes fixed on you—
and we see who we are.
We are not poverty, to you.
We are not addiction, to you.
We are not retained to the past, to you.
We are not sanitized history, to you.
We are not a societal burden, to you.
Our culture is not mocked by you.
You see us as your creation and by you we are strengthened.
We are imago Dei, made in your image.

MARIAH HUMPHRIES, *VOICES OF LAMENT*

I'VE DONE NINETY-SEVEN FUNERALS in the first nine years at my established church. That is ninety-four more than I did in my eleven years at the church plant where I served previously. A mentor told me after the first few months of this that while I would get another Sunday to preach, I wouldn't get a second chance at a funeral, so I should show up, listen deeply, do my work, and serve generously.

The work of remembering is important in established churches. When you listen deeply to the stories of people, pay attention to the anchors of memory that tether the community to its shared history, and graciously receive these stories as a way to understand what the past can teach the future, you can remission with much greater precision and awareness. You can learn what traditions need to be extended and what sins need to be repented of for the sake of the community.

Funerals are opportunities to listen to and remember with a community about its location, rituals, symbols, hopes, dreams, and fears. One of my mentors, Michael Catlett, shared these questions to ask when meeting with families to plan a funeral:

- What five words would you use to describe the deceased?
- What gave them joy?
- What broke their heart?
- What made them laugh?
- If they had a free day with no particular responsibilities, what would they do?
- What did they like to read, watch, and listen to?
- What did they do for work? What did they do since they retired?
- What are some of your favorite memories of them? Why?

After ten funerals I realized that these questions were the same kinds of questions I needed to ask for my church in doing the work of remembering. Here are the questions translated into a church context:

- What stories do people tell about the church's glory days?
- What stories do people tell about its failures?
- What stories do people tell about their fears of the future?

- What symbols, rituals, programs, or events were connected to the glory days or the failures?
- What stories do people tell about their hopes for the connection of the past to today?

The work of remembering is a way to develop the relational capital that transformation requires in the remissioning process.

REMEMBERING WELL

Remembering is a theme that runs throughout the Scriptures: God beckons his people to remember his steadfast love toward them amid their despair and destructive behavior (Lam 3:19-23); God's people struggle to remember times when they were not enslaved (Deut 6:21); Christ invites humanity to participate in the Eucharist, habituating the practice of remembering how salvation is born from the grace of his life, death, and resurrection (1 Cor 11:23-26). The salvific event is the entire story of God's activity stretched out from the beginning of time until the consummation of all things, and it begins with remembering: remembering who is the Creator, who is this God who calls his creation into relationship and instructs them on the grace-filled ways to live. Salvation begins with remembering the story of God—not parts of it, or only the stories of the New Testament, but the stories throughout all of human history (and preceding it), where God invites all humanity and all creation into deep relationship, reconciliation, and a hope-filled future. The habit of remembering creates the possibility of a Christian imagination.

One of the unique contributions Christians can make within any institution, but especially our churches, is the practice of remembering well. Cultivating a good memory helps us avoid the pitfalls of thinking a church is incapable of failure or hopelessly incapable of creating value. Because we have been invited by the Creator of the universe to exercise a good memory, we can develop habits of remembering the times of both flourishing and failure as a means of imagining a new future and understanding the experiences of the present.

In the aftermath of the murder of George Floyd, a number of Confederate monuments were removed in Richmond, Virginia, near where I live. Our community engaged in many conversations about remembering our history and whether removing these markers of struggle, conflict, oppression, and war meant we were destined to repeat our mistakes. We discussed the need to intentionally examine our actual history and not how some people preferred to remember it. The two largest spikes in the creation and erection of Confederate monuments happened in the early nineteen hundreds and in the fifties and sixties. The influx of statues was influenced by challenges to civil rights in the United States—the early nineteen hundreds was the post-Reconstruction and Jim Crow era, and the fifties and sixties saw the post–World War II introduction of civil rights legislation. We often perceive statues as long-tenured and permanent, but we can usually find much more insight if we remember well.[1]

Christians can expand our emphasis on remembering the incarnation as a unique event in the salvific process to include the whole scope of Jesus' existence—the life, death, and resurrection of Christ—as a means of habituating our memories around significant creative-destructive moments in Christian history. Christians practice *anamnesis* (recalling the life-death-resurrection of Christ) regularly, remembering Christ's death in the Eucharist and entering the promise of new life in Christ with each experience of the meal. The practice of remembering helps us imagine how the Easter-shaped crucifixion stories of the church can be interpreted in the here and now.

Churches that practice remembering create a network of roots that facilitate sustainable and contextually appropriate growth. Beth Ann Gaede describes this process as "rooting":

> A time of rooting in tradition is meant to help the group form a "corporate memory" or "get on the same page" with their history. There seems to be a general myth in congregations that "everyone knows the story," which generally is not true. . . . Storytelling in spiritual discernment calls for putting all the pieces of the story together, so that everyone knows the "thicker" story.[2]

Rooting is the intentional art of remembering, the creation of a framework on which to imagine a collective future. Looking back and cultivating a common sense of history can build unity in the present while framing an institutional future.

Traditioned Innovation + Creative Destruction

The Rule of St. Benedict says you should "keep death daily before your eyes."[3] But remembering our mortality isn't easy, for people or churches. And the last thing an institution wants to talk about is death. Traditioned innovation avoids the temptation to render the past as utilitarian or describe the future as utopian. Greg Jones, originator of the phrase "traditioned innovation," explains how innovation will impact the institutional landscape:

> Sometimes that will mean we innovate within existing institutions; at other times we will allow some forms to die so that other ones can rise up in their place. And at still other times we will give birth to new forms to address challenges and opportunities. But even our most dramatic transformations ought to be tethered to our most life-giving past.[4]

The pressure for churches to keep death before them is an uncomfortable task, but without remembering the past, churches might become untethered from their own histories. Traditioned innovation depends on a heightened awareness of context.[5] Remembering can often feel like a kind of death—a tethering that limits freedom. Michael Jinkins in *The Church Faces Death* writes, "It would appear that following Jesus means giving ourselves over to him in such a way as to invite a kind of death, a freedom consisting in the denial of being—free to do as we wish."[6] In remissioning there is no context-less existence for a church. Language, *telos*, habits, and desire are all born out of a place and a people. There are no blank slate churches because there are no blank slate people.

Traditioned innovation and creative destruction are not synonymous terms, but creative destruction depends on a practice of traditioned innovation that urges destruction for the sake of new life. You can be innovative from the context of tradition without necessarily destroying, but creative destruction depends on the kind of innovation that urges the end of some practices so new life will be possible. Traditioned innovation may be an extension of a tradition or a resituating of a tradition in a particular context without anything old passing away. However, creative destruction is always the intentional and active practice of pruning old and fruit-squelching branches so that fruit might be borne.

When discipleship doesn't include the cross but is an escape plan from hell, participation in the slow-but-steady work of dying to new life seems unnecessary. Discipleship that takes seriously the invitation of the cross avoids the illusion that following Jesus should always be easy or fun. Churches that are interested in this kind of deliberate and incremental movement forward reveal the bankruptcy of those who try to rush ahead and break the bonds of community and tradition instead of finding a path toward a shared future with some degree of unity.

Can't Forget the Broken Parts

There is an art to receiving the past with humility, letting history speak into the present like a still, small voice in our ears.[7] Without the voice of history, we might forget the injustice, sin, and abuse committed by churches that have brought us to the modern impasse. Traditioned innovation is the art of knowing what can be redeemed, what must be cast aside, and what might be preserved. Jones writes:

> We do not need radical change. The task of transformative leadership is not simply to lead change. Transformative leaders know what to preserve as well as what to change. We need to conserve wisdom even as we explore risk-taking mission and service. Too much change creates chaos. Transformative change, rooted in tradition and the preservation of wisdom, cultivates the adaptive work that is crucial to the ongoing vitality and growth of any organism, Christian institutions included.[8]

Traditioned innovation helps us remember that there is no story, no person, and no institution outside the scope of salvation. The *telos* of traditioned innovation is not change but transformation, i.e., movement from brokenness toward restoration. The hope of God meets those who are brokenhearted, exiled, and religiously outcast as well as those who are obstinate, failed, and destructive—no one is past the reach of God's grace—so why not our churches too?

Redemption and restoration are made possible through the power of Christ who helps people, and therefore our churches, lay aside the sin that entangles us so new horizons of possibility emerge for the here and now as well as the future. People who practice traditioned innovation help us remember how our "capacity for sin points us back to the significance of institutions, revealing our need for the church to teach and train us, through faithful practices and holy friendships, to unlearn sin and learn holiness."[9] Traditioned innovation is a unique process of perpetuating tradition through an intentional awareness and remembering of the past so it might be properly translated and recontextualized into the present.

Traditioned innovation is faithful stewardship of the past in the same way the managers are tasked with multiplying resources in the parable of the talents (Mt 25:14-30). Perpetuating tradition isn't merely conservation for the sake of survival; rather, continuation of tradition is meant to be utilized and put to work for the sake of the greater good and so that it might be multiplied for the flourishing of all people and creation. Institutions in our communities represent the individuals tasked with multiplying the talents, and all will be held accountable to the cosmic manager when asked how they stewarded their resources of time, money, talent, and power. Destruction is burying talents in the ground and letting the talents waste away. Churches practicing traditioned innovation preserve for the sake of investment and mission rather than survival. When institutions practice traditioned innovation, the process can become a habit that creates boundaries for what faithful innovation looks like, simultaneously revealing what must be preserved and stewarded toward a new future.

However, remembering isn't easy, especially in the context of church sinfulness and violence. Sometimes we remember so we can faithfully innovate, but sometimes we remember so as not to make the mistake of believing we are incapable of the same horrors. Institutional memory depends on a kind of truth-telling and death, for "Christ redeems the past; he does not undo it."[10] The people of God have a long history of forgetting God, forgetting the faithfulness of God, and forgetting our own sinfulness in the midst of hardship, suffering, or injustice.

A faithful reception of tradition is a willingness to enter into the messiness of human history without washing our hands like Pilate—pretending it never happened—or believing that because it didn't happen on our watch, we are not responsible for the consequences of the institutions we find ourselves in today. Christian participation in any church must be serious about the art of remembering, for it will necessarily involve the practice of forgiveness as we "attend to the wounds of memory and consider how they are healed in Christ."[11] Stewardship and faithful reception depend on an intentional practice of remembering the good and the sin so we might carefully and hopefully orient ourselves toward a future marked by the resurrection and restoration of all creation. The art of remembering helps us develop the "moral imagination to put ourselves in the shoes of other people,"[12] which is an essential tool to cultivate habits of faithful traditioned innovation. If Christians cannot be truth-tellers in their institutions, practicing confession, forgiveness, and reconciliation, then "who will tell the stories so that people don't forget?"[13] Faithful reception of tradition and its context is letting go of the myth that we are a people who can choose our own stories or pretend there were no stories before ours.

ASK REMEMBERING QUESTIONS

Once, an elder leader from my church said in despair, "I'm not sure there will be a church for my children, grandchildren, or great-grandchildren. I just don't know what to do." This person isn't alone. Some folks feel like their church is dying and there is nothing they can do about it.

Earlier in this chapter I shared questions that can help with funeral planning but that also run in the background of your established church's collective mind. As your church changes, some will think it is dying. The questions in the chart below can help you remember well and cultivate stories of the past that help inform your future. Remembering well will help you honor the past without glorifying it. People will have different answers to the questions, but if you do the work to remember well, you will find consistent themes to help you both continue in the spirit of the best of your tradition and repent from the brokenness of your past. A faithful imagination for the future relies on remembering well. As my mentor shared with me: show up, listen deeply, do your work, and serve generously.

The church I pastor has a campus on the railroad tracks that run through the center of our town. Our original building still has the wood floors that were laid at its founding. During the Civil War our church campus served as a hospital for both Union and Confederate soldiers. There are still bloodstains on the wood floors that mark that time in our history. In more recent times of conflict in our church and considering the hostile political climate, remembering our past role as a healing station for warring parties helps to inform our work in the community today. The saints before us laid down their political preferences to bring healing to soldiers and remind them that faith prioritized over politics allows the lion and lamb to lie down together. But to be a hospital in times of pain means you must be present in times of conflict that are not solved quickly. Use table 10.1 to help your church remember well so its future learns wisely from its past.

Table 10.1. Remembering to remission tool

Remembering questions	Remembering stories
What happened during the glory days of our church?	
What were some of the worst days in our church?	
What do you fear we might lose as we go into the future from our past?	
What were some important programs, events, people, or rituals our church shared together?	
What elements of the past are still present today that you hope we will hold on to?	
What are some of the changes that have happened over the years that helped the church become healthier and more faithful to the mission?	

FURTHER READING

Samuel Freedman, *Letters to a Young Journalist*, rev. ed. (New York: Basic, 2011).

Beth Ann Gaede, ed., *Ending with Hope: A Resource for Closing Congregations* (Lanham, MD: Alban, 2002).

L. Gregory Jones and Célestin Musekura, *Forgiving as We've Been Forgiven: Community Practices for Making Peace* (Downers Grove, IL: InterVarsity Press, 2010).

Michael Jinkins, *The Church Faces Death: Ecclesiology in a Post-Modern Context* (New York: Oxford University Press, 1999).

11

BURYING PREFERENCES FOR THE SAKE OF MISSION

We do not think ourselves into new ways of living.
We live ourselves into new ways of thinking.

RICHARD ROHR, "JOURNEY TO THE CENTER"

ON AUGUST 20, 1979, to many people's surprise, Bob Dylan, the longtime folk singer-songwriter, released his nineteenth studio album laced with themes about Christianity, God's love, and impending judgment for people who proclaimed they loved God but didn't act like it.

To be honest, I grew up listening to Dylan as a child and I couldn't stand him. My dad loved Dylan's songwriting and we often listened to his hits while driving down the road. Songs like "Mr. Tambourine Man," "All Along the Watchtower," "The Times They Are a-Changin'," and "Blowin' in the Wind" were played loud and I learned to sing them riding in my dad's Ford Escort. One of the best things about these songs for someone like me is that even though I can't sing my way out of a paper bag, I probably still can sing better than Dylan!

Sometime late in high school I finally began to appreciate my dad's love for Dylan. I remember singing "Gonna Change My Way of Thinking" off that first Christian-themed album. The first verse starts like this: "Gonna change my way of thinking / Make myself a different set of rules."[1] From the time I was a kid until now as an adult, these words have resonated as simple and profound truths: I need to change my way of thinking and live by a different set of rules.

It's actually a good definition of repentance: a change in the way we think and measure success, a change in how we live and what influences us. But for our established churches, repentance requires more than a change of thinking. For too long we have been content in patting ourselves on the back because we have been open to shifts in our thinking without bearing fruit.

When Fertilizer Doesn't Work

In Luke 13:1-9, Jesus addresses two tragic current events that for his audience must have been the talk around the proverbial water cooler of the day:[2]

> At that very time there were some present who told him about the Galileans whose blood Pilate had mingled with their sacrifices. He asked them, "Do you think that because these Galileans suffered in this way they were worse sinners than all other Galileans? No, I tell you; but unless you repent, you will all perish as they did. Or those eighteen who were killed when the tower of Siloam fell on them—do you think that they were worse offenders than all the others living in Jerusalem? No, I tell you; but unless you repent, you will all perish just as they did."
>
> Then he told this parable: "A man had a fig tree planted in his vineyard; and he came looking for fruit on it and found none. So he said to the gardener, 'See here! For three years I have come looking for fruit on this fig tree, and still I find none. Cut it down! Why should it be wasting the soil?' He replied, 'Sir, let it alone for one more year, until I dig around it and put manure on it. If it bears fruit next year, well and good; but if not, you can cut it down.'" (NRSV)

One event is a state-sanctioned terrorist act, and one is a random accident. In both stories, people's lives are snuffed out with little warning and for no apparent reason. Both events would have had people scratching their heads, their hearts full of questions, thinking about how precarious and fragile life can be. Jesus implies that the people who were killed were no worse than anyone else. They weren't the sinners of all sinners or the vilest of the vile. They hadn't done anything specific to cause their own demise. We can imagine that at this point Jesus might try to defend God. He could try to convince folks that God manages the tragedies of the universe quite well. But that isn't the direction Jesus takes.

Jesus implies that we shouldn't equate tragedy with divine punishment. Sin doesn't prompt God to cause great atrocities. Hard things simply happen. Life is fragile and often feels rushed and urgent. Jesus seems to hear the crowd's anxiety about these two difficult and tragic events, and he turns their attention away from the disasters, victims, and "why" questions and toward those still living. Jesus turns to those of us who have survived the hardships and hazards of the universe and what society has brought our way. He wants us to be careful not to mistake our good fortune as a special blessing from God. To do that would be to imply that bad fortune is a punishment from God.

Instead, Jesus orients the conversation around repentance. The need for repentance is a universal condition. Random victims need it just as much as folks who survived the event with fingers crossed. We all need to repent—to change the way we perceive ourselves, God, and each other. Jesus responds to both tragic situations with the same answer: unless you repent, you will all perish as they did. Jesus recognizes the horror of both the massacre and the accident, and he's not afraid to stress the suddenness of death or the unpredictability of life.

If Jesus ended the story there, we might think he's just like every fire-and-brimstone preacher we've heard on TV or seen characterized in movies. But Jesus doesn't stop there. He follows a different path. He doesn't promise freedom from calamities, but he does urge his listeners to be wary against false assurances that things won't happen to them because they sin less than someone else. It's like the story about the two hikers in the woods. They come upon a bear, and the two friends look at one another and get ready to run. One hiker pauses to slip on his running shoes. His friend says, "You know you can't outrun that bear with running shoes, right?" The first hiker says, "I don't have to. I just need to outrun you!" Life isn't like some great race to sin less than our friends or neighbors so God gets them first! But many churches are tempted to measure their success, viability, and *telos* against other churches instead of the life-death-resurrection motif of Jesus. Instead of a *telos* aimed toward cosmic reconciliation and human flourishing, institutions can be content with self-preservation (keeping the lights on) until the end of the journey.

AVOID THE RACE TO THE BOTTOM

When churches race to the bottom, everyone loses. The people of God, who have been rescued from oppression and sinful institutions (Egypt, Babylon, the Roman Empire, and even their own Israelite kings), are invited to repent and participate in another kind of kingdom. Christians must find a way to embody habits oriented toward the flourishing of all creation. An institution aimed at being slightly above the bottom rung of the ladder undermines its own value and removes itself from a participation in clusters of shared value. Seth Godin writes:

> Let's not race to the bottom.
>
> We know that industrialists seek to squeeze every penny out of every market. We know that competitors want to drive their costs to zero so that they will be the obvious commodity choice. And we know that many that seek to unearth natural resources want all of it, fast and cheap and now. . . .
>
> *But the problem with the race to the bottom is that you might win.*
>
> You might make a few more bucks for now, but not for long and not with pride. Someone will always find a way to be cheaper or more brutal than you.
>
> The race to the top makes more sense to me. The race to the top is focused on design and respect and dignity and guts and innovation and sustainability and yes, generosity when it might be easier to be selfish. It's also risky, filled with difficult technical and emotional hurdles, and requires patience and effort and insight. The race to the top is the long-term path with the desirable outcome.[3]

The race to the bottom for institutions is not embodied out of the narrative of Jesus' downward mobility (see Phil 2:3-11) but an expression of self-preservation and a habit of selfishness at the expense of others.

In the parable following the two stories of tragedy in Luke 13, the tree that has been cared for without bearing fruit is a symbol of unrepentance. Unless the fruit tree begins to produce fruit, it will meet its just and swift destruction. Jesus makes a startling claim in this parable: just as we shouldn't think our sinfulness brings tragedy, neither should we think that simply existing means we're bearing fruit. Just because a church hasn't been cut down doesn't mean it's living the good life or bearing fruit.

The parable emphasizes that it is Christ's continual patience and mercy at work keeping the axe from the tree. The owner of the vineyard has found the tree without fruit for year after year, but the gardener pleads, "Please, let me get the soil ready; let me give it fertilizer." Churches are like trees and God is like a great gardener, doing everything possible to get the soil of our churches ready to bear fruit. God never leaves us to our own resources but fertilizes our landscape with love to bring about fruit and repentance. The question for our churches is: will we bear fruit with enough time to thwart the axe? Creative destruction is marked by repentance (pruning and death) that leads to restoration (fruit and life). Keeping the lights on isn't enough. Destroying resources for the sake of profit isn't enough. Having money in the bank is not enough.

Life is fragile and urgent, not because God is out to get us, but because when we repent and reorient the way we see God, our own sin, and each other, we can bear good, nutritious, life-sustaining fruit for the here and now. Repentance is a gift from God and a habit that makes fruitfulness possible. Like pruning, repentance may be painful, but that doesn't mean it's an obligation or burden. Repentance is a gift, i.e., an opportunity to reorient our love in the right direction. God carves out a beautiful opportunity to show us incredible graciousness despite the hard things life brings us.[4]

Mission First

One of the most formative practices your church can engage in to remission is to regularly bury your preferences for the sake of a greater mission. Regularly give up some of the things you prefer collectively so you can find new ways to bear fruit.

There is an episode of *Radiolab*, a podcast that describes itself as being on a "curiosity bender," that describes how trees of different species living in a forest have an underground network that allows them to share food, nutrients, and resources so that they might all live. It's called the "Wood Wide Web."[5] We might expect trees to grow stronger and taller and block out trees of other species, sizes, or age, but instead they are caught up in a network of relationships.

In forests there are eyelash-size threads in the soil that can measure miles and miles long connecting trees to each other. While we might assume the tree's roots are what provide the tree with nutrients, it's actually this small tube-like fungus connecting the trees that helps them receive nutrients from the soil. In return, the trees make sugar to help the fungus live. Eventually the fungus and the roots intertwine, the tubes wrapping themselves into the root system so tree and fungus can work together.

What's even more beautiful, complicated, and amazing than this (check out the whole episode if you get a chance!), individual trees will use the fungus to communicate when they need more nutrients, minerals, or resources. The trees can also send warning signals to each other through the fungus. They send a chemical into the fungus that's like a cry of pain or danger, and the fungus helps them produce a chemical that makes them taste bad to an attacker (say an invasive beetle). But here's the most amazing part:

> SUZANNE SIMARD: As those trees are injured and dying, they'll dump their carbon into their neighbors. So—so carbon will move from that dying tree. So its resources, its legacy will move into the mycorrhizal network into neighboring trees. . . .

> ROBERT KRULWICH: When sick trees give up their food, the food doesn't usually go to their kids or even to trees of the same species. What the team found is the food ends up very often with trees that are new in the forest and better at surviving global warming. It's as if the individual trees were somehow thinking ahead to the needs of the whole forest.

> SUZANNE SIMARD: So we know that Douglas fir will take, a dying Douglas fir, will send carbon to neighboring Ponderosa pine. And so why is that? . . . There's an intelligence there that's beyond just the species.[6]

There is something profound in the way God has created trees to be caught up in an inescapable network of mutuality.[7] Trees need each other. Trees look out for each other. Individual trees lay down their lives for trees that come after them and are more equipped to withstand current pressures and long-term issues. Whatever affects one tree directly affects all of the trees indirectly. If even trees can die with purpose, how might our churches be more intentional to invest ourselves in a future we may not ourselves enjoy? If trees can bury their preferences for their own lives, their own species, and their own well-being for the sake of the whole and for those trees coming after them, how much more purposefully and intentionally can we in our churches learn to bury our preferences for the sake of the mission God has for us? When we fail to live this out together we short-circuit the development and discipleship of our people.

One of the common ways established churches learn to bury preferences is by moving from a Sunday-centric discipleship plan to a gathered and scattered plan. Many churches create discipleship opportunities before and/or after the worship service on Sundays: youth, children, and adults all meeting in classes before worship created convenience, easy ways to track participation, and a collective experience. Other activities would happen on Sunday evenings. However, as youth sports, schools, and other extracurricular activities now occur regularly on Sundays, churches are discovering that when a family misses a Sunday they miss . . . everything. When the gathered rhythms of a church's life are confined to one day, it leaves out a host of families who are not able to participate in worship and discipleship groups weekly.

Many churches have learned to bury their preference that Sunday be the only day for discipleship opportunities. This means that previously left out or unconsidered families can have an opportunity to experience community and discipleship. In my church this looks like having some core programming on Sundays (worship and some discipleship groups) while multiplying the number of scattered discipleship groups that meet during the week and different times of day. We have groups based on age as well as affinity. We also create one-page discipleship guides connected to the Scriptures we use in worship as a way to foster connection to one another even when we can't be in worship together. These discipleship guides can be used by individuals and groups to create community and shared spaces for the Spirit to work even while scattered.

Disrupting the status quo of Sunday-centric worship and discipleship can frustrate some church members because it reveals the loss of a time when church was experienced as a central part of a person's week and rhythm of life. Burying the preference for Sundays to be the end-all-be-all of making disciples often reveals other unnamed expectations (e.g. worship attendance as the governing metric to define success, Sunday School as the "proper way" to pass on the faith, and groups that meet during the week don't "count").

The language of "burying our preferences" for the sake of our shared mission is language we can use in every area of work. Too many mission opportunities? How might we bury our preferences together and prune where necessary so we can bear healthier fruit? Unclear discipleship pathways? How might we bury our preferences together and prune where necessary so we can bear healthier fruit?

Burying our preferences is a helpful way to shift disciple-making from creating consumers to developing citizens of the kingdom. Practically, the process follows these principles:

- Set limits. Establish an agreed-upon time frame for a program, event, or format to bear fruit.
- Talk directly about preferences and the need to lay them down for a shared mission.
- Give people space to identify preferences and grieve losses.
- Put manure on it, i.e., give something a chance to bear fruit before you prune it or cut it down.
- Situate burying preferences within the bigger story of how God transforms us. (It's not just change for change's sake!)
- Create opportunities to reflect on the experience of burying preferences and invite people to share what they have learned.
- Encourage people to live it out before they decide if they believe it.

As a leader, be honest about how you are burying preferences in your own personal life and in your shared life at church. (Most people will assume that everything that happens in worship, discipleship, and so on is your preference!)

Burying your preferences as a church will help you practice repentance with your whole life. And it will create a clearer pathway to communal transformation.

FURTHER READING

Richard Rohr, *Everything Belongs: The Gift of Contemplative Prayer* (New York: Crossroad Publishing, 1999).

Wendell Berry, *Jayber Crow* (Berkeley, CA: Counterpoint, 2001).

Willie James Jennings, *The Christian Imagination: Theology and the Origins of Race* (New Haven, CT: Yale University Press, 2011).

Henri Nouwen, *Peacework: Prayer, Resistance, Community* (Maryknoll, NY: Orbis Books, 2005).

Amy L. Sherman, *Agents of Flourishing: Pursuing Shalom in Every Corner of Society* (Downers Grove, IL: InterVarsity Press, 2022).

12

EVERYTHING IS LITURGICAL
(SO REMISSION ON PURPOSE!)

God be in my head and in my understanding.
God be in mine eyes and in my looking.
God be in my mouth and in my speaking.
God be in my heart and in my thinking.
God be in mine end and my departing.

DIVINE HOURS, SARUM PRIMER

Solidarity with the world means full commitment to it, unreserved participation in its situation, in the promise given it by creation, in its responsibility for the arrogance, resultant distress, but primarily and supremely in the free grace of God demonstrated and addressed to it in Jesus Christ, and therefore in its hope. How can there be any question of a generous view and understanding apart from this participation? The community which knows the world is necessarily the community which is committed to it.

KARL BARTH, *CHURCH DOGMATICS*

CAN YOUR MEETINGS, BUDGETS, and administrative tasks be a training ground for discipleship? Sometimes we look right past meetings for finance, personnel, deacons, greeters, or event setup and miss the opportunity to equip and support leaders. Whether we realize it or not, every time we meet with people we are in a discipleship and formation process. Remissioning churches and leaders learn to see each of their administrative teams, volunteer events, behind-the-scenes groups, budget committees, and other tasks as primary ways to disciple people who have already committed to serve instead of looking elsewhere for the "real" work of ministry.

One of the biggest shifts my church has made in its budgeting process has been to extend the timeline and heighten collaboration. The budgeting process begins in February and wraps up in October. We utilize our budgeting process to clarify our priorities, seek opportunities to collaborate across ministry areas, and match our financial resources with the mission. Since everything is formation, what does it look like for your church to remission on purpose?

Training Grounds

Churches are the places where people gather to order their loves and orient their desires.[1] Even before we can think about why churches matter, we experience the purpose of churches by the practices we embody. These practices are a means of shaping our hearts, giving us a vision for the kingdom of God and helping shape the *telos* of our gathered community for the sake of the world.

James K. A. Smith begins the first of his books on cultural liturgies by naming how our life is formed:

> If education is primarily *formation*—and more specifically, the formation of our desires—then that means education is happening all over the place (for good or ill). Education as formation isn't the sort of thing that stays neatly within the walls of the school or college or university. If education is about formation, then we need to be attentive to all the formative work that is happening outside the university: in homes and at the mall; in football stadiums and at Fourth of July parades; in worship and at work.[2]

There is no place we can go, no institution we can participate in, that can keep us from experiencing a formation that develops our desires. Whether we are shopping in a mall, voting in an election, going to church, joining a gang, volunteering in a civic club, or eating at a restaurant, participating in institutions develops our habits, and those actions shape the fundamental ways we pay attention and live in the world.

Churches are the places, the organizations and shared spaces, where two or more gather to worship, serve, and bear witness to God. We gather as churches to share in practices and develop habits that train our hearts to love. The institutional practices we embody and participate in give insight about what matters most to each of us and to our communities. Churches are the never-ending boot camps of our hearts.

Critical to understanding how churches function in this way is to understand the precognitive habits that reveal the *telos* of where love is directed. Smith says, "What distinguishes us (as individuals, but also as 'peoples') is not *whether* we love, but *what* we love."[3] Our communal practices orient our vision of the good life and motivate us by giving us dispositions for how we should act without having to think. When people ask me if I believe miracles still happen I say, "Yes! The fact that any church exists amid our propensity to treat each other poorly and yet choose good is a miracle!"

Relying on the work of philosophers like Aristotle, Aquinas, and Mac-Intyre, Smith describes how our dispositions—our precognitive tendencies to live in certain ways toward particular ends—are developed by habits. "These habits constitute a kind of 'second nature': while they are learned (and thus not simply biological instincts), they can become so intricately woven into the fiber of our being that they function *as if* they were natural or biological."[4] Churches develop habits to help people love in a particular way and toward a particular end without having to stop to think about it.

What habits does your church already have that could be reconstituted or reimagined so you can more fully live into your mission? Where are people already living that they can be redeployed with more purpose?

I've seen this happen at my church with the team of people who care for the property. Both the building and the grounds are taken care of by a lot of generous volunteers. One of my favorite things is to pull up to church on a weekday morning and see two of our volunteers catching up and laughing at something in their group text message—while sitting on lawn mowers. A couple of the leaders have been wise to invite people to join who are looking to serve but don't want a front-facing task involving a lot of people. These leaders recognized that even though they could accomplish many of the tasks on their own, the real magic happens when they share in the work, form relationships, and laugh together.

Don't Waste Meetings and Documents

There are two things I never imagined learning this much about in my pastoral career: one, the maintenance and cost of HVAC units, and two, the value of updating documents regularly to serve your team and church. I don't have much nice to say about HVAC units except they are great when they work and expensive when they don't! But learning to value the process of discipling people via documents and committee meetings was a surprise to me. I've come to see that good policies and procedures are incredibly important (e.g., family leave policies that support staff who are starting families, clear personnel manuals in case of discrimination) because they are acts of hospitality, especially in times of crisis.

Meetings don't have to be worthless, and organizational documents don't have to be a waste of energy. What if each committee was an opportunity to cultivate and practice the full breadth of APEST? What if the creation and revision of organizational documents was a tool that enabled conversations about mission, vision, habits, and theology? What would it look like for you to include as part of your committee/team/leadership meetings a layer of discipleship that helped your already-showing-up leaders grow and develop for the sake of the larger mission?

Here are a couple of ideas about how to be more intentional about committee meetings:

- Include a ten- or fifteen-minute discussion of leadership, discipleship, or mission the committee can live into or applicable to an issue you are facing together.

- Create a shared practice that will help the committee see its work together as an overflow of faith and part of a larger ecosystem. (Are there preferences that must be buried?) For example: fast, practice a particular kind of prayer, exercise, read, reflect on Scripture.

- Practice APEST, i.e., include a diversity of voices representing apostle, prophet, evangelist, shepherd, and teacher. If it's not possible to have all of APEST represented, take time in meetings to think about what the missing voice(s) might say.

- Spend time with the leader and apprentice before meetings and invest in them personally. See the work of the committee and their leadership in the context of formation.
- Connect the committee's work to its *telos* as often as possible.
- Don't complain about meetings, and show up prepared.

Similarly, your organizational documents at their best help articulate and contextualize your church practices in order to shepherd internal relationships and release you for mission. Too many documents read like reactionary documents designed to contain poor practices; as a result they maintain fear instead of perpetuating healthy communication and relationships. Also, organizational documents should not be used as a substitute for engaging with people relationally. Emphasize the need for people to interact personally before institutionalizing a response.

Here are some questions to ask as you are working to become more intentional with your organizational documents:

- Is the document a list of "do-nots" or does it set a bar of helpful expectation?
- If someone from outside your organization read the document, what would they say about it?
- What values are clear from the document? What values are missing?
- Who does this document benefit? Who loses?
- What are the processes for reconciliation or correction when issues arise?
- If you could start over with the document, what would you change? What would you keep the same?
- Are the most vulnerable in your midst protected in your documents?
- Is a common language and vocabulary shared across documents?
- How can you make the process of creating and revising a document a means of discipleship?

It is possible to see meetings and documents as a process of growth and leadership development instead of a drain on the system. If you can slow down enough to recognize that the people who have said yes to serving in those groups and reimagining your documents are being formed by how you guide them, an extra step to think about their formation could be a tremendous gift to your church.

FROM BUDGETS TO MISSION FUNDING PLANS

Remissioning churches shift from thinking of budgets as amoral documents to seeing them as a clear way to demonstrate commitment to mission. How would you describe the way your church builds a budget? Is it an open process? Who is involved? What story does your budget tell? Budgets are one of the ways our neighbors can clearly understand what our churches are about. Numbers make it difficult to lie. They tell the story of priorities and emphases. What would it look like to shift your budgets to mission funding plans?

Remissioning churches also learn how to summarize their mission funding plans in an accessible way for all people in your church to understand. I ask my staff and leaders to work incredibly hard on summarizing, highlighting year-over-year shifts, and explicitly describing how their budget documents reflect a commitment to chasing our mission and practicing our values. Then we have them show their work and build the mission funding plan with a team, so these teams can grow the vision, understand the practices, and chase the mission together.

We take plenty of time to work on this together each year. It was an act of traditioned innovation to shift from thinking about simple dollars and cents, income and expenses, and instead realize that the real work is to pray, plan, discern, seek resources, and connect the dots to the mission God has put on our heart—to do much more than simply keep the lights on. The following text shows an example of the summary page each ministry area submits.

MISSION FUNDING SUMMARY PAGE

Objective

The objective of this **$<Enter Total Budget>** funding proposal is to articulate the amount of funds needed to resource the <Name of Church> mission related to <enter ministry area> for calendar year <year>.

Goals

The goals for the use of these funds are to cultivate unity, hospitality, neighboring, wholeness, and honoring in the ministry areas that relate to persons our church identifies as <Enter ministry area> (ex. youth, college aged, and families). These missional postures (unity, hospitality, neighboring, wholeness, honoring) are meant to express how congregants live on mission at our church but encompass the current priorities of the <enter ministry area> ministry.

Highlights

(Be sure to highlight differences between years; include why you are highlighting additions and subtractions—this helps stewardship know what is upcoming and highlights importance.)

(Ex. increase in college ministry program funding from $1,000 in 2017 to $3,000 in 2018 to support new on-campus programming.)

- Enter Budget Highlight
- Enter Budget Highlight
- Enter Budget Highlight

Missional Postures (Church Values)

- Unity: We are one community made up of unique individuals.
- Hospitality: We care for others and try to put ourselves in their shoes.
- Neighboring: We treat our community like family.
- Wholeness: We pay attention to our spiritual, physical, and emotional well-being.
- Honoring: We respect the past while nurturing the future.

Unity = $ <enter unity funding>
Hospitality = $ <enter hospitality funding>
Neighboring = $ <enter neighboring funding>
Wholeness = $ <enter wholeness funding>
Honoring = $ <enter honoring funding>

Mission funding plans are another opportunity to disciple leaders and help them connect the "why" and the "how." When we take the time to do this well, we also make room for the business leaders in our church to think intentionally about the way they steward their own resources and grow a culture committed to mission.

EVERYTHING IS LITURGICAL

Ultimately, all actions, documents, meetings, gatherings, fun events, times of conflict, and so on form us into the church we are and hope to be. Instead of propping up the church-industrial complex, how might you see church administration and operations as liturgical—the work of the people— that shapes who you are becoming together as the people of God infused by the Spirit? Don't you want your policies and procedures for working with minors to reflect God's heart for the vulnerable in your midst? Isn't discerning how to work with support organizations that serve people in need a worthwhile endeavor? These aren't a waste of time. Our documents, budgets, meetings, and structures can help protect, serve, and give infrastructure for our churches to grow in a healthy way.

One reason established churches fall asleep at the wheel is they stop seeing the connection between their faith and their shared work as the people of God. Do you really want people managing church finances if they aren't praying for your church? Do you really want people making personnel decisions if they aren't reflecting on Scripture and seeing their decisions as an overflow of their faith? Do you want documents that reflect business practices but have no space for reconciliation or forgiveness? Since when did it become okay not to expect spiritual growth and maturity? When we lead meetings and create policies that are "just business" but have nothing to do with how we follow Jesus together, we create a gap between leadership character and leadership positions. People are allowed to serve with or without marks of the Spirit in their lives.

There is no rule that meetings have to be lifeless. There is no reason your documents can't express hope and guide people towards maturity. Everything you do as a church shapes who you are and who you are becoming. What steps can you take to be more intentional in that formation?

FURTHER READING

Charles Duhigg, *The Power of Habit: Why We Do What We Do in Life and Business* (New York: Random House, 2012).

Phyllis Tickle, *The Divine Hours* (New York: Oxford University Press, 2007).

Dietrich Bonhoeffer, *Life Together*, trans. John Doberstein (New York: Harper & Row, 1954).

PART FOUR

DEVELOPING DISCIPLESHIP PATHWAYS

Producing kingdom fruit looks like an identity rooted in becoming more like Christ, committed to a sent community of people who are demonstrating Jesus' love, and being on mission together for the sake of the world.

EUN STRAWSER, *CENTERING DISCIPLESHIP*

Can we seriously believe that God would establish a plan for us that essentially bypasses the awesome needs of present human life and leaves human character untouched? Would he leave us even temporarily marooned with no help in our kind of world, with our kinds of problems: psychological, emotional, social, and global? Can we believe that the essence of Christian faith and salvation covers nothing but death and after? Can we believe that being saved really has nothing whatever to do with the kinds of persons we are?

DALLAS WILLARD, *THE DIVINE CONSPIRACY*

13

THE FOUR SPACES OF BELONGING IN A REMISSIONING CONTEXT

Leadership is energizing a community of people toward their own transformation in order to accomplish a shared mission in the face of a changing world.

TOD BOLSINGER

AT AN ESTABLISHED CHURCH I VISITED, I was moved by the way people talked to and treated each other as family. There were hugs, handshakes, laughs, and a strong sense that the church wanted people to feel welcome and experience kindness. The worship service was clear and there were good instructions throughout the service about how to participate.

Shortly before the message, the pastor went up to the pulpit to lead a time of prayer. The prayers reflected that week's prayer list distributed by the church. A major difference, however, was that the prayers led by the pastor filled in the details that had been left off the list. They discussed the kinds of infections people were battling. They included descriptions of the surgeries people had endured, including graphic details of the recovery process. There were clear indicators of families working through marital issues. Some of the prayers pointed to people's financial challenges.

Nothing malicious was said and the prayer time didn't come across as gossip. However, sharing personal details for more than ten minutes of a worship service where many guests were present created an unintended effect—guests felt like they were on the outside looking in. It was a misuse of the public space designed to help people belong. Remissioning churches need to look closely at the ways they gather people and serve them with intention.

Robin Dunbar, a British evolutionary psychologist, has shown that the number of stable relationships anyone can maintain at once is 150. He points out that while our whole social network may be larger, our cognitive limits max out at 150 based on our ability to maintain social connections involving trust and obligation.[1] This helps explain one of the major challenges of churches struggling to grow beyond two hundred people: there is cognitive difficulty in knowing how to maintain connection in a church when it grows beyond any one person's ability to know everyone.[2]

DISCIPLESHIP IN THE FOUR SPACES OF BELONGING

Remissioning churches must think creatively about how to intentionally build discipleship pathways in different spaces that share in the broader mission. In his book *The Search to Belong*, Joseph Myers states, "Space isn't empty; it is rich with meaning and plays a major role in shaping your relationships."[3] According to Myers, there are four kinds of spaces—intimate, personal, social, and public—and they each create different possibilities and limitations for how relationships function. In all four spaces we connect, are committed to participate, and find the connection significant.[4] Inspired by Myers, along with Eun Strawser, JR Woodward, and Dan White Jr., figure 13.1 shows a way to think about the four spaces of belonging in a remissioning context.[5]

FOUR SPACES OF BELONGING IN REMISSIONING

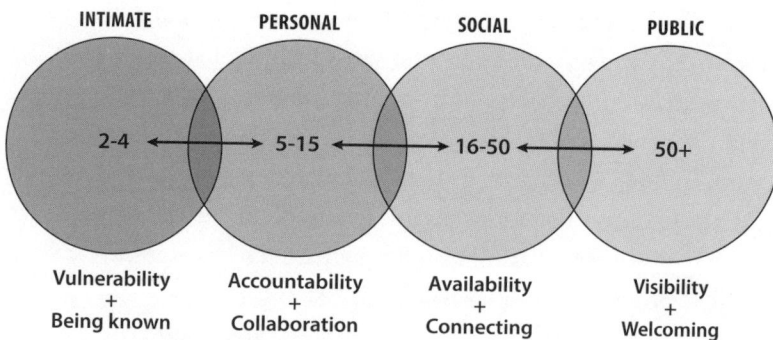

INTIMATE	PERSONAL	SOCIAL	PUBLIC
2-4 ⟷	5-15 ⟷	16-50 ⟷	50+
Vulnerability + Being known	Accountability + Collaboration	Availability + Connecting	Visibility + Welcoming

Figure 13.1. Four spaces of belonging in remissioning

While missional church planting networks emphasize growing disciples before they start gathering in public spaces, most established churches don't have the freedom to get discipleship "right" before starting social or public space groups. So what are the opportunities and challenges for established churches as they think about making disciples in each of these spaces of belonging?

The arrows between the spaces of belonging help remind us that in discipleship pathways, people move between the spaces. Some will start in intimate space and make their way to larger groups with different purposes, and others will begin in public space and move into more personal space in time. Mapping the spaces where people find belonging helps us create meaningful invitations and challenges to grow as disciples.

Since many established churches already have each of the spaces of belonging, it's helpful to remember that people can find entry into community in any of them. Regardless of entry point, remissioning leaders need to help people learn to move into other spheres of belonging through intentional discipleship. How can you help someone who has connected in the intimate space to enter the public sphere, where you gather with people who are different from you and learn to follow Jesus through a practice of welcome?

In a conversation among leaders of established churches in the US and UK, each of the leaders discussed their challenges in guiding people into different spaces than they may be comfortable with. People often cherish the low accountability of public space but resist the vulnerability of being known in intimate space. Others like personal and social spaces but feel like a small fish in a big ocean in the public space. Helping people learn about the spaces of belonging diminishes the pressure to make every event or gathering achieve the same relational goals. It also gives language to discuss how we all have preferences for what we see as "home base" in the spaces of belonging. This has become a practical way to ask people to take up their cross in order to cultivate healthy spaces of belonging in their church.

Remissioning in the Spaces of Belonging

Remissioning churches learn how to create different programs, events, and discipleship pathways to help disciples mature and live on mission together using the different spaces of belonging as a guide. Too often, established churches over-rely on one or two spaces to do all of the work. How can your church structure events, programming, and activities that create pathways to belong in each of the spaces?

Public space. The public space is what most established churches think of as "church." It is often the public worship service that folks consider their public space. This is the largest discipleship space, usually with fifty or more people (although if your church doesn't have fifty people in it, that's okay! You can create public spaces by joining and collaborating with others).

The public space certainly is one way disciples are made, and it is an important way. But one challenge is that it's usually based on one-sided communication. It lacks personal, vulnerable, and in-depth interactions because of its size and scale. The greatest temptation in this space is to emphasize the public gathering above all else and create religious consumers who participate only passively in the other spaces—if they participate at all.

The public space is not meant to create deep bonds or relationships rooted in accountability. One of the greatest challenges for remissioning churches is to stop expecting intimate relationships to develop in the public space and to stop allowing the numbers and resources of the "worship experience" to determine the church's success or viability. Numbers and participation in the public space can be high even when transformation is next to nothing. Attracting a crowd does not mean you have a church of disciples.

Still, the public space can be a tremendous opportunity to train leaders, disciple people into exercising their gifts, celebrate diverse abilities, and proclaim the good news. The hope of the gospel is a public hope. Jesus and Paul both spoke to large crowds to invite people into a kingdom way of life with Jesus as Lord. It's interesting to note that for both Jesus and Paul, the visibility of the public space got them in trouble with oppressors and the religious establishment.

The public space is important, and it creates a welcoming environment where people can get to know the tone, atmosphere, and hospitality of your church. Public space gives credibility and an opportunity for people who are interested in the kingdom to experience a taste and receive an invitation into the imagination of Jesus for our world. But we must be mindful not to expect the public space to do the challenging and long-term work of transformation in the same way that a core discipleship group can do in intimate or personal spaces.

Social space. The social space is rooted in an understanding of the Greco-Roman household. This household consisted of the immediate family and extended family living in close relationship together with other relatives, servants, employees, and even close friends of the family. The social space is sixteen to fifty people, the average size of a church in the New Testament. Most American churches have less than a hundred people and would have been relatively large compared to churches in the New Testament era.[6]

Social spaces provide a wonderful taste of authentic community and are large enough for people to do scalable mission work together. In this space there are enough people to share the load of the work and begin to develop deeper relationships. This gathering of people is a way for folks in the community to see a foretaste of the kingdom, where diverse people are living out love and relationships in meaningful ways.

The social space often works well around geography or context, whether it is a shared neighborhood, geographic location, or network of relationships, where connections can develop without force. The social space is rooted in availability—that is, rooted in a context where people can naturally expect to encounter one another and have relational proximity.

The social space is not where confession or accountability can realistically take place. Social space is at its best when it garners greater relational connection because of proximity (be it geographic, network, shared interest, etc.). The social space is fruitful when people are connected, are able to know one another's names, can care for one another as illnesses or celebrations arise, can spend time together as families and friends, and enjoy one another's presence with each person participating in such a way that their voice, contribution, skills, and gifts are valued and have room to work.

Personal space. The personal space is meant to reflect the twelve disciples Jesus invited to follow him closely and learn his way of life. These relationships are deeper and good for accountability because of the limited number. In the personal space a leader can invite others to join in a way of life where we mutually learn to live like Jesus in our neighborhoods and join in the mission of God. In this space people can reflect, dialogue, and interact with greater responsiveness.

In the personal space we invite people to live out a common rule of life and share in habits that help us have eyes to see, ears to hear, and practices that encourage us to live out the mission of God. In this space accountability and belonging can and should take place. In this space the confession of sin, exploration of hopes and dreams, and challenge to live out the mission are interconnected. And it is where we are linked to the social space where we live, work, and play.

The personal space is not isolated from intimate, social, or public space. Our relationships overlap as we move from one sphere into another. But the people who make up the personal and intimate space are our discipleship core. These are the people we spend the most time with and who we learn the most from as we participate in mission together.

In remissioning contexts, personal space is often missing. Sunday school classes and discipleship groups are often lecture- or teacher-oriented and lack meaningful places to dialogue and interact. It took seven years for some of the senior adults at my church to be comfortable with this space. They had known people for twenty to thirty years but never been vulnerable or created a sense of belonging together. When our seniors embraced personal space, they learned new ways to include each other and guests who often struggled with loneliness and grief.

Because of the accountability and depth associated with personal space relationships, be mindful to create processes that foster reconciliation, conflict navigation, restoration of brokenness, and healing with grace.

The farther you move from public space into intimate space, the greater the vulnerability and accountability become and the more intentional you should be about challenging people to live out the cruciform life with each other. While that invitation can be issued in the public space, it is the personal and intimate spaces where the challenge is practiced with regularity, accountability, and appropriate vulnerability.

Intimate space. The intimate space is modeled after the relationships Jesus had with Peter, James, and John, who followed Jesus the most closely. In this space are the deepest levels of mutuality, intimacy, and vulnerability. These relationships should be born out of the social and personal spaces, but be mindful of the human proclivity to pursue homogenous relationships instead of the diverse relationships that are characteristic of a healthy discipleship core.

The intimate space is made up of folks you can share coffee, a beer, or a meal with to continue the conversation and equip each other to lead in other spaces. There should be a high degree of mutuality in the way discipleship happens in this space. There is both accountability and vulnerability in how shared practices of communion and community inform the practices of co-mission.

There are important guidelines to be aware of in this space. Because of how vulnerable these relationships are, they should be with people you trust and who trust you. These people should know the truth about each other without shame or fear of judgment. This doesn't mean the relationships are perfect, but they should be marked by vulnerability and the grace to grow. Depending on the emotional and spiritual health of the people participating, you as a leader may need to help this space grow and develop over time, until you sense in the Spirit that it's safe and appropriate for the relationships to be boldly vulnerable.

COLLABORATIVE DISCIPLESHIP

Many of these spaces exist in established churches, but they often lack the intentionality necessary to make them reproductive and multiplicative. An important question to ask regularly is: which space are we trying to multiply and why? How do we help people move into spaces where they've not yet experienced belonging?

Collaboration works best when you have a discipleship core in the intimate and personal spaces that helps build healthy social spaces, which then create incarnational public spaces, rather than building an attractional public space aimed at helping sheep from other churches purchase your religious goods and services.

If your social and public spaces are struggling, it's because your intimate and personal spaces need attention and intentional discipleship work. Social space is the sphere where new personal and intimate space leaders can be discovered, but that means you and your leadership need to be intentional in developing relationships in your social space and not only in public worship gatherings.

Instead of trying to overhaul your entire church system, focus on one of the spaces of belonging and grow the infrastructure to support meaningful relationships. And use existing places of belonging that are working well to talk about the other spaces you are trying to mature. For example, in one established church that had a vibrant worship service, meaningful social space, and steady intimate space, leaders were noticing a generational drop-off in personal space groups. Their existing Sunday school classes for boomers and older people were well-attended, but millennials and younger people weren't attending. This in turn was affecting the attendance of children and youth for discipleship groups before worship.

The first thing the church tried was to double down on inviting younger adults, youth, and children to attend Sunday morning pre-worship activities and creating a welcoming culture for them. However, after a year of trying to make things work, attendance remained low. Instead of trying to sort things out on their own, the leaders gathered a group of young adults who were regularly participating in worship, serving in mission pathways, and demonstrating commitment to the church but were not attending a Sunday morning personal-space-sized discipleship group. They discovered that the desire existed, but the methodology didn't work. Between sports, caring for aging parents, school commitments, travel for work, and their hectic pace of life, these young adults preferred personal space groups that offered more than one hour to grow relationships before worship and could meet on a day of the week less affected by extracurricular activities. This church decided to change its Sunday mornings to allow for more flexibility and a communal rhythm that wasn't contingent on worship attendance. Worship attendance didn't decrease, but young adult participation in personal-space discipleship groups grew dramatically.

Here are a few questions that can help you assess your own church's spaces of belonging:

- Who are the people in each space? Write down their names. Can other pastors and leaders on your team identify these people as well?
- Which people are functioning as links between the spaces?
- Where are you spending the most time trying to multiply disciples? Is it working? How do you know?
- Who are the apprentices learning to lead in each space?
- What happens when you try to be vulnerable in the public space and visible in the intimate space?
- Which of the four spaces do you find the most comfortable?

- Which of the four spaces do you find the most challenging?
- How can you link your discipleship core to your social space for mission?

Collaboration for mission is the heart of discipleship. Our communion with God connects us to one another and to the networks of relationships that foster our place of mission. What would happen in your church if you were intentional about making disciples in these four spaces?

FURTHER READING

Angie Ward, ed., *The Least of These: Practicing a Faith without Margins*, Kingdom Conversations (Colorado Springs, CO: NavPress, 2023).

L. Rowland Smith, ed., *Red Skies: 10 Essential Conversations Exploring Our Future as the Church* (Cody, WY: 100 Movements Publishing, 2022).

14

CREATING SHARED EXPERIMENTS TO GROW A REMISSIONING IMAGINATION

Love made me an inventor.
MAGGY BARANKITSE

WHAT IS THE ONE THING people tell you not to change when you arrive at an established church? That's right, worship. But why not? Is it because people will get angry? Resist the change? Is changing worship really any different than trying to change a missions partner or adjust where money goes in the budget?

When I arrived at my first senior pastor position, the worship services were a major source of pain and disconnection. We had a "contemporary service" that met at 8:30 a.m. with no activities or programming for young families and sang songs from the 1980s. There were about seventy-five people in a sanctuary meant to hold six hundred. The traditional service drew a few more people, but for all these hymns people "loved," I couldn't hear anyone singing except the choir or music director. There was a rigidity about adhering to a script more than being sensitive to anything the Spirit might be saying. And the more on time we finished so we could get to lunch or the golf course, the better. Was this really the best we could imagine for our public space of worship? Why do we fear leading change in the actual places where people are gathered?

HOSPITABLE ECOSYSTEMS

Churches that participate in habits of creative destruction and traditioned innovation become what artist Makoto Fujimura describes as "cultural estuaries."[1] Estuaries are the places in a waterway where saltwater mixes with fresh water, forming a unique habitat for the various plants and animals particularly suited for that environment. Estuaries act as a buffer where some fish lay their eggs so they can more easily swim downstream after birth, or particular kinds of animals that are more directly in competition become interdependent on other species for survival. The purpose of an estuary then is "not so much protection as preparation."[2]

Estuaries help build strength and competition between various species and increase the capacity of animals and plants for better participation in the ecological culture. The Hudson River estuary in New York Harbor depends on oysters to filter the water, even turning some pollutants into pearls. They can filter only a certain amount of toxicity before becoming toxic themselves. The oysters prepare the estuary to be an estuary, taking in some death so life and relationships in the river can thrive. Christians in churches (and other institutions) have this same call—to die with the pollutants so the entire ecosystem might live. Helping the diversity of churches flourish "moves beyond mere tolerance to respect for the other in the context of our common life . . . [into] the macro vision for stewardship that cares for the overall system and respects many types of contribution."[3] Cultural estuaries are clusters of shared value where simply being in the system brings benefit, and Christians within those ecosystems must function like oysters, taking pollutants out of the water and restoring the water to greater health. The filtering process for Christians participating in various institutions can build a movement with macro implications:

> Movements don't emerge because everyone suddenly decided to face the same direction at once. They rely on social patterns that begin as the habits of friendship, grow through the habits of communities, and are sustained by new habits that change participant's sense of self.[4]

The habit of filtering, taking out the old so the newly restored might flourish, alters the ecosystem of institutional involvement and begins to model the habits of creative destruction. Christian participation in creative destruction within institutions helps reframe the starting point and *telos*: "the starting point is to recognize that change is not a threat. It's an opportunity."[5]

In my church, worship was the estuary. It was the place where the most people were gathered, and people wanted it to be meaningful even if they didn't know how to change. One of the reasons people are so resistant to change is they don't know how the transition will work and lack common experiences to point to together for reference points as they mature and navigate the change together. Worship services are a helpful place to create common experiences of change together. Worship was not the place to make bold claims about controversial issues, but it was a place where we could learn to be uncomfortable together in trying some new habits and to pray for a heart to love our neighbors instead of thinking only about what made us comfortable in worship. Where else does your church purposefully gather, sing songs, listen to a message, pray, and create a shared experience other than worship each week? My church recognized that navigating change in worship wasn't a threat; it was one of the best opportunities to grow together.

SKUNKWORKS

The word *skunkworks* was born when the US government hired Lockheed Martin to create a jet fighter faster than Germany's in 180 days or less in 1943. There were time constraints: 180 days; a clear mission: create a jet fighter that would fly at six hundred miles per hour; a formation-oriented process: engineers and mechanics with shared values and work ethics; and it occurred outside the building: the creation of the jet fighter happened in a rented circus tent outside the normal complex.[6]

Skunkworks is a way of renewing the center by working at the edges. Using the estuary metaphor, skunkworks are the experiments that happen at the edges of the brackish water to help give greater clarity and renewal in the salt or freshwater core. In church life, skunkworks are the high-risk experiments that can help propel your church into new space but present minimal risk to the overall church ecosystem. For Lockheed Martin, creating a new jet fighter in such a limited time and unusual environment was incredibly risky, but the experiment wouldn't lead to the shutdown of all Lockheed Martin projects if it failed.

Skunkworks are passionate, adventure-filled projects that can help your church explore new territory, bring disruption to the center through experiments on the margins, and, if successful, lead to a renewal of your church. The name also betrays its risks: these experiments are often smelly, risky, out-of-the-norm projects that are meant to shake things up a bit, like prophetic smelling salts for your senses.

One of the reasons churches often resist trying new things is they fear failure. Take a moment to work through the learning from failure reflection exercise in table 14.1 to help take the sting out of this kind of risk, knowing you've failed before and are still here!

Table 14.1. Learning from failure reflection

Describe a situation where you failed. Thinking back to the cultural exegesis charts in chapter six, list some of the components at play in the description of the failure.	
What disappointed you most in your failure?	
What is something you learned from your failure?	
What were some important programs, events, people, or rituals our church shared together?	
If you could give advice to your former self about the project, experiment, work, etc., what would you tell yourself to do differently?	

SKUNKWORKS AS SHARED EXPERIMENTS

There are four typical characteristics of skunkworks that enable them to provide the necessary experimentation space to renew the center from the margins in your established church. These characteristics are: time-bound, mission-centric, formation-oriented, and context-informed. The more you can conduct these kinds of experiments at the margins of your community, into the brackish water where your church's mission life meets real life, the better your chances of renewal.

A case study. The church where I currently serve conducted a shared experiment that involved all four of these elements, which helped it have a skunkworks flavor along with traditioned innovation and creative destruction. After a period of discernment, we went on a high-risk, time-bound journey birthed out of experiencing worship in different contexts than our own. This journey helped us reexamine how we made disciples and grasp a clearer sense of our mission.

Originally, we had a "contemporary" service at 8:30 a.m. meant to reach young families (because young families are stoked to get up for an 8:30 a.m. worship service with no childcare or kids' activities) and a "traditional" service at 11 a.m. with Sunday school in between. Neither service was working. Both were declining in number and lacking diversity.

Our leaders spent time praying, discerning, remembering, and imagining what the road forward might look like. A group of about sixty decided together that we would bury our preferences for worship styles, times, and dress to create a new path together. We moved from two services to one that included elements of worship from both services, as well as new elements not previously included in either. We changed the time for our discipleship and introduced new formation opportunities. And we took the formality of dress down a notch (our church was notorious for being a wealthy, white, country-club church).

We had folks get mad about all kinds of things (I didn't wear a tie, the new schedule interrupted their golf tee time, worship styles, and much more). But in the first twenty weeks, we had over thirty new people join the church, and we baptized children and senior adults. When it was time to decide whether we should stay with one service or go back to two, the church business meeting was packed with people who voted to continue to practice burying their preferences and grow in unity instead of worshiping around style preferences.

Time-bound. In this twenty-week experimental worship journey, both the 8:30 a.m. contemporary service and 11 a.m. traditional service met together at 10:15 a.m. (with a discipleship hour before) in a service that combined elements from each worship service but also introduced some new elements. We placed a time limit on the journey, and we couched the process in experimental language. The journey would take us to the margins of our normal worship experiences, but we would discuss at regular intervals—and then again at the end of the process—whether the experiment was bringing renewal at the center. At the end of the twenty weeks we would gather to discern what we had learned from the experience and seek lessons for renewal.

Often in established church contexts it is helpful for people to know that there is an escape plan. Placing time limits on the experiment reassures people that it will end if they really can't stand the change. It relieves some of the anxiety and helps people focus on the experiment at hand.

Mission-centric. The most crucial element of skunkworkery (I think I just made up a word) is that it helps you focus on an aspect of mission being neglected by the way you currently practice life together as a church. For us, this meant we were honest about how we were treating people differently based on how they were dressed. So I stopped wearing a tie in worship—not because I hate ties, but because of what ties represented. They were hindering our ability to shed our identity as a country-club, white, and wealthy church.

It shouldn't have been a surprise, but once the tie came off, I then heard about my pants being too tight, my need for a haircut, whether I had put on a few pounds or lost some, and about a hundred other things. The worship journey involved us shedding some literal outer layers to make room for healthier growth. Most important, it helped us see that worship should be practice and training for mission! Worship for the glory of God should lead to a greater sense of mission, not larger holy huddles isolated from the world. This ultimately led us to spend more time in our neighborhoods, go on more prayer walks, hold more listening sessions, and invest in more relationships. We brought new prayer requests and possibilities for mission into our worship, and then we sent people into those places.

We were clear throughout the process that the changes in time, dress, and worship content were to help us see each other and our neighbors with greater clarity. One of the major features of our new worship service was the introduction of a "prayers for the people" section, where we intentionally wrote prayers together for our church, community, nation, and world that named the particular pressure points our people were experiencing together.

Formation-oriented. The worship journey we went on was geared toward helping people take seriously the idea of discipleship as formation for life and mission. We preached and taught through the book of Acts to learn what it means to be church and how our actions shape who we are now and who God is inviting us to become. The worship journey involved over sixty people in various groups who helped us think about the "why" of worship and the ways our different practices shape us as individuals and as a collective. Before, worship had been a going-through-the-motions service on Sunday mornings. There was little life or understanding of why we did what we did. In our experiment we were ruthless about asking the "why" question over and over and thinking about how our shared practices were forming us, blinding us, lulling us to sleep, or sparking our imagination.

It led to the creation of a new "sending out" statement I wrote on behalf of the church, which has shaped how we think of the benediction (see figure 14.1). In fact, we call it the "sending out" instead of the benediction as a reminder that the end of a worship service isn't the end of worship or service.

Context-informed. Our worship journey began with experiences outside our church building in a few different contexts with diverse people groups. These worship experiences helped awaken the desire within our leadership to take a risk with our own central worship space. We visited a church that worshiped with an organ, piano, guitars, drums, and lots of other instruments alongside those. We experienced new ways of communal prayer that mixed singing and praying together. We introduced new voices to our context from the outside that helped reframe what was happening on the inside.

A shared experiment that helps you be a good neighbor and develop a clearer sense of mission is best if it is informed by what happens outside your normal context. We gained confidence learning from other churches so that when we raised the stakes to conduct this experiment in our Sunday morning worship journey, we had real-life examples to point to for proof of concept. Normally, skunkworks and experiments should happen farther out at the margins to minimize risk until you are able to build some trust and move

Figure 14.1. Our church's sending out statement

the experiments closer to the center. The risk increases dramatically, but the renewal at the center happens faster when the gap between the margins and center are bridged.

CREATING SHARED EXPERIENCES THROUGH EXPERIMENTS

Some people fear change because they lack the imagination to see, taste, or feel what the adventure will be like. I realized in my established church that nearly three-quarters of the folks hadn't experienced worship outside our denominational context in their entire lives. No wonder words like "contemporary," "modern," "technology," and "innovation" scared the daylights out of them! They had no framework to imagine another way of worshiping together.

When you create shared experiences through experiments, you allow the feelings of fear, trepidation, and loss to transfer onto the experiment, which gives you space as a leader to walk alongside and *with* your people. The experiment gives you a common experience to base your discernment on rather than imagined boogeymen coming to steal their church.

Shared experiences lead to new discipleship conversations and habits that create bridges of trust to walk across for the sake of a bigger mission. Here are three questions that are helpful to keep in front of you as you seek to create new culture with shared experiments:

- What skunkworks or edge experiments could you undertake to renew your center without traumatizing it at the same time?
- Could you start an intentional missional community who act like scouts, helping give you a clearer sense of the gap between your established church and your community?
- How can you incubate some fresh imagination and tangible experiences in your context?

Creating shared experiments helps disrupt and bring people along with you at the same time. Use table 14.2 as a guide.

Table 14.2. Creating shared remissioning experiments

Questions to guide planning	Responses
What is the mission of this experiment and how does it connect to our overall mission as a church?	
How long will the experiment last?	
What other contexts can we learn from to gain clarity in our own church?	
How will this impact the kinds of disciples we are making as a church?	
Who needs to be involved in the planning, execution, leadership, and communication of the experiment?	
How do we plan on communicating updates, learnings, and results of the experiment with the larger church?	

FURTHER READING

Makoto Fujimura, *Culture Care: Reconnecting with Beauty for Our Common Life* (Salem, MA: Fujimura Institute and International Arts Movement, 2014).

Clayton Christensen, Michael B. Horn, and Curtis W. Johnson, *Disrupting Class: How Disruptive Innovation Will Change the Way the World Learns* (New York: McGraw-Hill, 2008).

Maggie Barankitse, "Love Made Me An Inventor," Faith & Leadership, Duke Divinity School, September 12, 2011, www.faithandleadership.com/love-made-me-inventor.

15

MOVEMENTAL DISCIPLESHIP FOR REMISSIONING CHURCHES

*The courage it takes to rebuild the fabric of our community is the price
we pay for creating a world we want to inhabit. In the end, the way
to get past our discomfort is to do it again and again and again.*

PETER BLOCK AND JOHN MCKNIGHT, *THE ABUNDANT COMMUNITY*

WHEN PASTORS ARE CONSIDERING whether to join the thirty-week
Remissioning Collectives that help them apply remissioning principles to
their local context, one of my first questions is, What do you hope will happen
in your church because of your participation in this group? Many pastors
tell me they want to grow disciples, see flourishing in their community, and
make a difference in people's lives. It takes a little time to discover that an
underlying expectation is that they will also use these remissioning principles to grow their church numerically. There isn't anything wrong with a
church growing. But lots of things grow that aren't necessarily healthy or
good—our bodies grow cancer, after all. One church I worked with had
discipleship groups that met during the worship service because they didn't
like the pastor. They grew numerically while creating division spiritually.
Another church's discipleship groups collected donations for their Sunday
school classes so they could bypass the church budget.

Movemental discipleship looks at a church's discipleship processes against the backdrop of Jesus' invitation to participate in the kingdom of God. Examining our discipleship processes can bring up resistance, because personal and intimate space groups are usually the most connected and committed spaces in a church. They function like microchurches and, depending on the health and maturity of the leadership, they can be helpful or harmful to the overall life of the church. How do you create communal discipleship processes and shared outcomes while also changing how discipleship happens in your church?

AVOIDING TEMPTATION

In Alan Deutschman's *Change or Die*, the central premise is that although we can change our behavior, we rarely do.[1] For example, when patients suffering with heart disease are presented with the pathways for healing, ninety percent do nothing and choose to die, or they treat symptoms that do not fix the root cause. Deutschman says we often try to motivate change with fear, facts, or force. But people rarely change with those motivations. They may vote a certain way, buy a product, or give in to a fad, but long-term sustainable change rarely happens through these pathways. If it did, losing weight for the sake of our health would be a lot easier.

Fear, facts, and force rarely produce lasting, sustainable change in our churches either. Yet your church may be relying on these means of inspiration with its own people. Use the remissioning motivation assessment in table 15.1 as a guide to help you identify if this is the case.

Table 15.1. Remissioning motivation assessment

Questions to guide planning	Responses
Which motivation does your church tend to use to inspire or lead through change: fear, facts, or force? Give an example.	
Which motivation do you tend to use in your own leadership to inspire change: fear, facts, or force? Give an example.	
Describe the long-term effects you perceive as a result of fear, facts, or force being used to motivate change in your church and your own leadership.	

So what does make change possible? Deutschman says it comes down to relating, repeating, and reframing. Relating is finding new relationships that encourage you to keep learning and growing as a person. Repeating is putting into regular practice the habits that will help you be healthy. And reframing is being willing to see things from another perspective.

How is your church helping people relate, i.e., develop new relationships that foster growth and encourage them to walk with God for the sake of the world? What regular practices are you repeating, and are they producing the kind of transformation that bears fruit? When people want to give up, how resilient is your community to learn from and reframe failure? Where do you see possibilities when others see cul-de-sacs? How might you consider relating, repeating, and reframing as ways to produce lasting change?

Deep, Wide, Long, and High

The evaluation of discipleship in many established churches centers on numbers and participation rates. *Movemental discipleship*, on the other hand, considers the entire ecosystem of discipleship in a church to foster movement for the sake of community. Movemental discipleship considers how to mature a group of people as a collective without losing sight of the individuals that make up the church. Churches often miss the forest for the trees by only thinking about how to satisfy the needs of individual classes or people instead of asking how to create a movement with the whole of the church.

Are your discipleship pathways deep, wide, long, and high? To engage with the breadth and depth of what it looks like to follow Jesus and create belonging in our established churches, we must create space for disciple-making to happen:

- **Deep.** Movement takes place when Spirit-filled discipleship drives the impetus for church planting and when there are as many new births as transfer numbers.
- **Wide.** Movement is rooted in presence and incarnation moving fluidly between various geographic locations through relationships—local, regional, national, and global—which means mission is not just out-sourced to the experts!

- *Long.* Movement lasts beyond the tenure of senior leaders and becomes part of the DNA and formation of disciples in your context with sustainable rhythms.

- *High.* Movement cost is high, requiring risk, intentionality, creative destruction, listening, a spirituality of weakness, and finding identity in God, not reputation.

Here are some helpful questions for your established church to ask:

- What does movemental discipleship look like in your context?
- How are you discipling the whole person?
- What are some meaningful ways to measure fruitfulness?
- How can you measure sentness?
- What is currently being reproduced in your context? What would you like to see reproduced in your context?

Being intentional about discipleship and its pathways takes time, discernment, and regular recalibration. The goal shouldn't be to set it and forget it. Over the first five years of remissioning, there will be regular tweaks and at times major shifts until you find a rhythm and the right tools to help discipling happen in contextually appropriate ways. Contextual appropriateness is not only determined by what sticks in your church context but also how disciples are connecting in their neighborhoods and community.

If we connected deep, wide, long, and high movemental thinking to the four spaces of belonging, what would an intentional discipleship structure look like for your church? What is working for you? What is missing?

One church overhauled its approach to discipleship by changing their expectations. Instead of meeting weekly on Sunday mornings at the church campus, they moved into a family's home. They changed the rhythm to include social space opportunities where people could easily invite their friends, and they found existing programs in their community for service rather than having to make a mission opportunity themselves.

Maturity Pathways

Movemental discipleship isn't aimed at simply growing numbers of people involved in your church and its programs. It is about making space and creating pathways for people to mature from their starting point into fruitful imitators of Jesus.

And movemental discipleship doesn't occur only in discipleship groups. Movemental discipleship happens when discipleship is the underlying commitment in any event, program, or mission pathway. For example, one medium-sized church had a strong commitment to food access work in its community. For years people showed up to their food pantry to distribute food and restock the shelves afterwards. This church watched leaders and volunteers alike burn out as needs and demands grew in the community. The pastor recognized that the food panty leadership was getting stuck in its maturing process because there had been little emphasis on apprenticing leaders, connecting faith to social impact, and growing friendships among the people who served. After doing an inventory of how the relationships worked for those serving in the food access ministry, the church added a community garden to grow food together, made time to pray every time the food pantry was open, and shared meals together as volunteers to grow their friendships. The food access work has spun off several discipleship groups by incorporating discipleship into its framework of serving together.

How is your church discipling the whole person? What about different generations of people? Does someone have room to grow from immaturity into maturity? How do you help people live into the values and mission of your church? Most churches use one or two categories to make disciples: biological (age-based groups) and sociological (values-based groups, usually described as "new member" classes). However, to create mature disciples we need to consider other categories and then practically describe how we will make disciples in that framework.

Table 15.2 describes four cultural categories and invites you to consider what means of discipleship you are deploying to support people across age (biological), faith experience (holistic), belonging in a particular church (sociological), and service (spiritual). Remissioning churches will move beyond the initial recognition of a problem—such as a gap in leadership from one generation to another—and move to the practical by examining the means of discipleship (i.e. what curriculum is being used, what space of belonging is being deployed, is it a class or small group, and is the length of time working?). Use table 15.2 to map out the different pathways your church uses to disciple people in your context. Then, discuss with your leadership what gaps exist to disciple people into maturity.

Table 15.2. Pathways to discipleship

Cultural Category	Functional Category	Pathway	Means of Discipleship (content—what resources; spaces—intimate, public, etc.; mediums—class, small group, etc.; length of time—does it end, seasonal, etc.)
Biological	Age-based	Cradle to grave	Content, spaces, mediums, length of time
Holistic	Faith-based	Not yet—new—mature	Content, spaces, mediums, length of time
Sociological	Values-based	Not yet church—family	Content, spaces, mediums, length of time
Spiritual	Leader-based	Apprentice to leader	Content, spaces, mediums, length of time

Movemental discipleship relies on your church intentionally making room for the Spirit to shape people to live up, in, and out. Movemental discipleship is not a fast process in established churches. People have taken years to become the disciples they are today, and no one really changes overnight.

In remissioning churches, we tend to overestimate what will happen in the first three years and we far underestimate what is possible in the first ten years. As you think about creating movemental discipleship in your church, what is a realistic time frame for helping your church remission? Remission is a long, slow work headed in a particular direction. It's essential to recalibrate expectations around the length of time it will take to see sustainable transformation.

Movemental discipleship is at the heart of what it will take for your church to remission. Remember that Christianity began with a small group of people, faithful over many years and in the face of persecution, who followed Jesus with their whole lives and yet were not perfect. Movemental discipleship is not powered by you but by the Spirit. So as you open yourself up to that movement as a leader, you create more space for your church to grow.

ECCLESIAL ARCHITECTURE

How many [insert your denomination/association/political word here] does it take to change a light bulb?

There's a sting of truth in this joke because it hints at the challenges of our organizational structures and the way our institutions often stand in the way

of efficiency and change. In the remissioning process it is important to de-
centralize leadership and learn to become more thoughtfully structured
toward mission. Decentralizing leadership away from the senior pastor is
not about creating an absence of leadership but empowering a culture of
shared leadership. If we don't share leadership then we can't complain when
no one else leads because there wasn't room for them in the first place!

Thinking through the way your ecclesial architecture works is a complicated process. Depending on your context, denomination, and culture, some
aspects of your architecture might be set in terms of polity and governance.
However, discipleship pathways that exist in various governance structures
can help you navigate a long, slow obedience in the right direction.

Ultimately, this section is designed to help you examine the structure of
your church and ask, What kinds of disciples does our ecclesial architecture
create? Answering this question—in concert with the truth that our churches
are perfectly designed to get the results they're currently getting—can help
create healthy disciple-making churches that discern wisdom together.

A number of different archetypes have arisen over the years. Some reflect
the denominational charism, others reflect cultural adaptation, others are
connected to family systems, and many churches are hybrids of multiple
archetypes with overlapping benefits and dysfunctions. It is important not
to read these archetypes as a one-size-fits-all reflection of your church. Take
time to examine how your church might have taken on some of these structural tendencies, and with heightened awareness decide to repent and walk
forward into new life together.

The club. Club churches create community through shared societal
markers of status, collection of membership dues, a collective sense of who
the "outsiders" are, and rigorous protection of identity. Club churches
function like any club—women's club, country club, golf club, fraternity—
that brings together a like-minded and like-cultured group of people. Oddly
enough, this kind of church can have a deep sense of "missions" in that it
will engage in projects, stay busy, donate lots of money, and serve other
people, but they often struggle to connect the mission of God to their
everyday life. They feed poor children in another country but want their
neighbors in their local economy to pull themselves up by their bootstraps.

Club churches are organized to protect the powerful among the group. Those who exemplify what "success" looks like find themselves in the decision-making groups and wield the most power. Churches organized like clubs want to know the boundary markers for who is "in" and who is "out." Symptoms of a club mentality are preoccupation with issues of dress, financial status, race, culture, and other markers of power.

One club church in Virginia rarely had difficulty meeting its budget, connecting people in worship, or welcoming new Christians in their midst. However, it struggled to have credibility with community leadership (government, nonprofits, and schools) because of the feeling of indifference they created for those outside of the club.

Civic organization. Some of the longest-lasting civic organizations were created as outlets for community engagement alongside the church. Instead of the church trying to "do" everything, civic organizations such as Rotary, Kiwanis, Lions, and so on, were created to supplement the work needed to serve local communities. Some certainly have had club-like mentalities around race and culture, but many were focused on the common good.

Civic churches are organized around projects, missions, and common good activities that are hard to argue against. They build parks, feed hungry people, mentor kids in local schools, and from all appearances are up to a lot of good! However, civic churches often come to need remissioning because the source of their efforts has become disconnected from the Spirit. Civic churches often focus on the project and miss the people along the way. Many civic organizations are facing the same challenges as established churches that have done a lot of good but who have struggled enormously to pass on the faith to the upcoming generations. One of the biggest signs of a civic church is an active elder population without any apprenticeship or process to disciple others into the work.

Perhaps the most difficult aspect of civic churches is that they are geared toward the common good, but often the "missions" are preference- and personality-driven by a small group of people or a member of the organization with more resources (money, power, political will, etc.). Many mainline denominations that have had an incredible social impact struggle to connect the dots spiritually to the "why" of their work. One of these churches broke the cycle of disconnect simply by creating a prayer list of each of the neighbors they served and praying for people by name instead of serving them and going home.

Family reunion. Churches like to take on the *Cheers* theme, to be a people where "everybody knows your name." In settings of a hundred people or less it is possible to know each person by name along with some basics about each family. There are some deep benefits to knowing the back stories, histories, tendencies, and habits of the various families who make up the church. Simultaneously, when a church functions like a family reunion week after week, many people may not understand the unspoken rules and traditions, which leaves them feeling unsure of how to engage in relationship. New people often must earn their family badge and are treated as outsiders to the family system.

There are plenty of images in Scripture of the church functioning as a family, but you'll notice there is also a strong emphasis on adoption and even leaving behind our fathers and mothers to be faithful to the mission. When churches are contingent upon a small collection of families to fund the church, make important decisions, and "sponsor" changes, there is a lot of trouble when the family system experiences divorce, sin, or a misappropriation of power over the rest of the church.

When a church functions like a family reunion, it often spends the bulk of its time telling stories of the golden years when its shared identity was being formed and it feels most alive when talking about the past. You'll notice that when other families start to arrive or connect more deeply into the life of the church and the weekly family reunion feels threatened, the original family will seek to flex its muscles to assert its leadership over the family system. It may flex those muscles with might, or it may undertake mindful political maneuvering as well.

CEO-driven church. Remissioning churches can become reflections of businesses that have emphasized decision-making efficiency over shared mission development. Churches don't have to be large to fall into this trap of elevating the senior leader or leadership team as the end-all-be-all decision-makers of the church. The greatest threat of this architecture is that it puts the responsibility of following Jesus on the leaders and paid staff and removes the expectation that everyone is living out of their own relationship with Christ. In this setting, the CEO and board of elders, directors, or leaders become the scapegoat for the church to lay its sin and issues upon while freeing the people from looking inwardly at their own sin and lives.

While churches that have a strong leadership from the top will often make faster decisions, the significant risk is the people become consumers of religious goods and services and expect staff to carry the weight of the work on their behalf. To the degree that the platform of the senior leaders grows without meaningful accountability, the roots of the church may shrink in depth and ability to sustain the plant for the long haul. While this model is one of the clearest signs of the church-industrial complex, it would be a mistake to think this model is alone in its participation.

Remissioning church. While every church has some shared characteristics of the best of these other archetypes, there are some unique characteristics of what makes church . . . well, church! And to remission your church will require special attention to what is unique about church amid all the institutional options available to people. In our polarized age, these characteristics help structure your church for mission. Remissioning churches:

- Emphasize kingdom citizenship over identity politics
- Are as close as family but don't lose a sense of self
- Reject the binary options of caring for the church and being on mission
- Avoid the binary options of CEO leadership and organized chaos
- Free up and empower APEST leadership
- Are centered around the apprenticeship of Jesus in all aspects of life

What marks of a remissioning church can you grow in your context?

STRUCTURED FOR MISSION

Now that we have examined some of the different archetypes of ecclesial architecture, it is helpful to discern what kinds of values are helpful in structuring for mission. What are some practices that help structure churches for mission and can be deployed in various committees, teams, vestries, boards, and other architectural environments?

Apprenticeship. What does apprenticeship look like in the context of your leadership, discipleship, committee, and emotional development spaces? How are disciples passing on discipling on your finance committee? How are Sunday school teachers developing future leaders? A culture of apprenticeship helps undercut the temptation of consumer Christianity. What could your small groups, committees, and teams look like if apprenticeship became an expectation for development? How might apprenticeship thwart the temptation to have lifelong leaders in positions without ever moving on? How might apprenticeship create a sense of passing the baton to various generations of leaders? How does a posture of apprenticeship shape your own leadership as you continue to follow Christ? Apprenticeship helps create a culture of shared leadership over time when leaders develop other leaders.

Informed by 3DM's life shapes (see www.3dmovements.com), figure 15.1 is a simple square that shows how to invite people into discipleship processes.

A simple application in my context has been how we run our committees. The leader (chairperson) and an apprentice work with the staff leader to plan for meetings, set goals, and connect spiritually. Don't waste existing opportunities to develop and apprentice people for the leadership they are called to and to connect that work to their imitation of Jesus.

Formation + information. Too often we focus on helping people have the right information to lead, teach, shepherd, and pioneer while neglecting their formation.

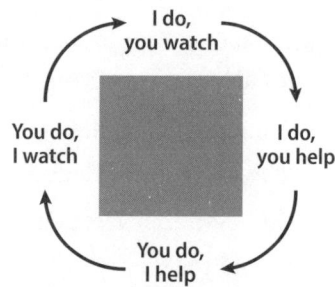

Figure 15.1. How to invite people into discipleship

What might it look like to develop our committees' and leadership teams' spiritual and relational lives as we equip them with important information for making decisions? How many problems would our people face differently if that were the case? Information without formation is a clanging cymbal. Remissioning requires churches to consider the formation of the people serving in positions of leadership as we help them accomplish the tasks associated with their roles.

Character + gifting. One church where I served wouldn't allow anyone to hold a public-facing role (e.g., worship team, teaching, community development, etc.) until they had served on the "trailer team"—helping set up and break down—for six weeks. The aim was to see what a person was like behind the scenes and on a team before placing them in leadership. Too often in established churches if a person is breathing and has gifts (can play an instrument, runs a business, served in the military), they are given a leadership position without any evaluation of whether they are emotionally or spiritually faithful. This doesn't mean you hold out for people with perfect character, but you do need people to be growing toward maturity. At best your ecclesial architecture holds character in tandem with gifting. But if you have to choose one, begin with character. An unhealthy leader can wreak lasting havoc on a group of people. Could you consider leaving a vacancy in a leadership position if there isn't someone with demonstrated character to fill the space? A good rule of thumb is to ask, Does this person's character match the leadership expectations of the position you'd like them to serve in? If not, might you find a space for them to continue to develop? If so, can you name with them the reasons their leadership character is so important?

Discernment over efficiency. Established churches are notoriously snail-like in their decision-making pace. Efficiency is important, and in many established contexts it can be a prophetic move to increase the speed of decisions. However, discernment is more important than efficiency. Discernment is about valuing wise decisions that will stick and lead to formation over checking a box. A good rule of thumb is to see how people's behavior changes after a major decision to see if it has been caught by the body. If your aim is formation of disciples in the way of Jesus, it is crucial to make decisions in a way that brings along the most people while also being careful not to avoid your most persistent question askers. Is your leadership environment like a bulldozer that clears the way no matter what is in front of it? Does your ecclesial environment have room to ask questions and grow into shared understanding?

It is important to think about how to begin the process of reforming your ecclesial architecture in the following ways:

- Define various leadership roles.
- Articulate the decisions that various teams, committees, and so on can make.
- Ask where the places of discernment are in your decision-making processes.
- Consider how you disciple character and emphasize formation.

- Create an environment where repentance is normal and possible.
- Think of committees, teams, vestries, and so on as disciple-making tracks.
- Use the four spaces of belonging to create deeper formation opportunities within your structure.
- Prune unfruitful committees and teams.

There is no perfect ecclesial architecture. Using traditioned innovation, creative destruction, and divine experiments, consider how you might create a healthy ecosystem where leaders can be apprenticed, the habit of discernment can be developed, and character can be shaped for the sake of your mission.

FURTHER READING

Alan Deutschman, *Change or Die: The Three Keys to Change at Work and in Life* (New York: Regan, 2007).

Peter and Geri Scazzero, *Emotionally Healthy Relationships: Discipleship that Deeply Changes Your Relationship with Others*, expanded ed. (Grand Rapids, MI: Harper-Christian Resources, 2017).

Alan Hirsch and Mike Frost, *The Shaping of Things to Come: Innovation and Mission for the 21st Century Church* (Peabody, MA: Hendrickson, 2003).

16

RACE, CLASS, AND THE KINGDOM OF GOD ARE ESSENTIAL FOR REMISSIONING

In Acts we find faith caught between diaspora and empire. Faith is always caught between diaspora and empire. It is always caught between those on the one side focused on survival and fixated on securing a future for their people and on the other side those intoxicated with power and possibilities of empire and of building a world ordered by its financial, social, and political logistics that claim to be the best possible way to bring stability and lasting peace.

WILLIE JAMES JENNINGS, *ACTS*

Racism isn't a math equation. It's a historical sin that remains a contemporary challenge.

KEN WYTSMA, *THE MYTH OF EQUALITY*

IN THE SUMMER OF 2019, I was nearly fired while navigating the complexities of race at my church and in my local community. I am a white, male senior pastor of a 165-plus-year-old church that sits just outside the former capital of the confederacy in Virginia. The remissioning process described throughout this book isn't just an abstract concept—it's a lived process. The church I serve and a sister church in our community have journeyed together by worshiping together, starting a nonprofit together, and serving with one another to see justice and reconciliation embodied.

In this chapter I invite you to consider that, scripturally and theologically, any church seeking to remission so the kingdom of God is on earth as in heaven needs to navigate issues of race and class. I will share the story of my church and how we learned we are not the heroes of the story God is writing in our community—but when we are receptive to the disruptive work of the Spirit that leads us to repentance, we can see kingdom breakthrough.

The arduous, important, and essential work of navigating race, class, and the kingdom of God is often seen as a secondary issue in the remissioning process. I hear pastors and leaders say things like, "Let's remission and learn to grow, and then we'll navigate the more complex issues of sin." However, there's an old saying from my Young Life days that has always shown itself to be true: "What you win people with is what you win people to." This mantra is why a gospel devoid of the cross produces consumers who leave church when discipleship expectations increase. A remissioning established church takes a hard look at what we've won people with and how it is shaping their ability to live out the simple instructions found in Micah:

> What does the LORD require of you?
> To act justly and to love mercy
>   and to walk humbly with your God. (Micah 6:8)

Using the Remissioning exegesis table with a few added questions (table 16.2 at the end of this chapter), I am going to discuss how navigating race, class (socioeconomics), and the kingdom of God are essential parts of the remissioning journey. I want to be clear, though, that these aren't the only "isms" you may have to navigate. Racism and classism are only two of the many challenges remissioning churches face. For your community it may be sexuality, gender, nationalism, and more. Whatever your church faces, I hope this chapter serves as a helpful guide, especially for majority-white groups who want to remission their church while avoiding exercising their prophetic voice. In majority-white churches, the prophetic voice is perceived as impolite and discussing things in public meant only for private conversations in the home. However, learning to speak the truth in love is an essential skill in remissioning churches.

The input here will need to be contextualized based on your position, community, and history. The pace and tone of the work will differ based on the role in which you serve, the cultural context (specifically in this conversation about racial and economic diversity), and the groundwork already laid. I do not pretend to be an expert on your culture or context, but I situate these recommendations within the larger scriptural and theological journey we share as followers of Jesus. The process of remissioning will look different in churches that are beginning from a place of oppression or marginalization.

For example, I learned from a caucus of Black leaders that remissioning often begins in their churches with first asking what must be held, protected, and maintained as part of Black church culture before asking what needs to be pruned or buried. Since the pressure is already so intense to assimilate to a dominant culture, it is important to practice traditioned innovation before creative destruction.

Awareness of racial and economic disparity has grown through apocalypse (unveiling), particularly through the deaths of Freddie Gray, Botham Jean, Breonna Taylor, Ahmaud Arbery, and George Floyd, along with the targeting of Asian Americans in Monterey Park, Half Moon Bay, and Atlanta in the summer of 2020. This awareness has elevated the need to address race, class, and the kingdom of God as part of the remissioning process. Wrestling with how race and class have informed our current church environment will help us to more faithfully answer Jesus' question: What good will it be to gain the world (numbers, money, resources, people) and yet forfeit your soul?

SCRIPTURAL JOURNEY

The church's birth in Acts and the visions of John in Revelation give us a taste of what the kingdom of God will look like when God's restoration plan is fully realized. In Acts 2 Peter preaches his compelling vision as the Holy Spirit erupts in their presence and the prophetic words of Joel are given new context:

In the last days, God says,
    I will pour out my Spirit on all people.
Your sons and daughters will prophesy,
    your young men will see visions,
    your old men will dream dreams.
Even on my servants, both men and women,
    I will pour out my Spirit in those days,
    and they will prophesy. (Acts 2:17-18)

How will we know that the Spirit of God is waking up our dying churches in need of remissioning? Our sons and daughters (people promised to us by God that there is a future!) will prophesy. Young and old will have visions and begin to dream dreams again. Even those considered on the outside of power will receive the Spirit and tell of God's mighty work.

The birth of the church is a helpful picture of where remissioning should be headed. Young and old, women and men, the poor and the diminished become the voices of God's activity in the world! This comes on the heels of the Spirit being poured out on people who heard the good news in their own native languages. The church is birthed in unity without the need for uniformity of culture. Each people group named in Acts 2 helps us remember that God sees our different cultures, and where our diverse languages once caused confusion and sin, through the great reversal of Christ's work they are now a sign of God's scope of salvation. Culture is not obliterated nor is God blind to differences: instead each person and place is a marker of God's expansive table.

We see this again in John's vision in Revelation 7:

After this I looked, and there before me was a great multitude that no one could count, from every nation, tribe, people and language, standing before the throne and in front of the Lamb. They were wearing white robes and were holding palm branches in their hands. And they cried out in a loud voice:

    "Salvation belongs to our God,
    who sits on the throne,
    and to the Lamb." (Revelation 7:9-10)

The vision of God's kingdom, where all things are restored to their intended wholeness, culminates in this larger-than-life vision of people from all places, languages, nations, and cultures gathered around the shared salvation that comes through Christ. If this is a vision of where things are headed, shouldn't our churches begin to reflect this kind of diversity today? Shouldn't we recognize that unlikely people finding community together under the lordship of Christ is a way our neighbors begin to discern what we mean by "church"?

Willie James Jennings in his commentary on Acts recognizes that while the vision of unity is compelling, we must recognize the twin traps of power and diaspora that can reduce the church's focus to, one, setting the boundary markers of who is in or out or, two, using church as a means to guard power and identity for ourselves.[1]

Remissioning churches begin with an end or *telos* in mind. It can be helpful to situate our churches within the existing story of Scripture as a guide to discern and measure our kingdom progress over time. Are we seeing that people from different cultures are able to hear and embody good news with us? Can the lion and the lamb lie down together in this place?

THEOLOGICAL JOURNEY

Especially in churches where white people or people with wealth sit in the decision-making seats of power, it is extremely important to look backward before trying to live forward. Latasha Morrison writes in *Be The Bridge*, "When we lack historical understanding, we lose part of our identity. We don't know where we came from and don't know what there is to celebrate or lament. Likewise, without knowing our history, it can be difficult to know what needs repairing, what needs reconciling."[2] One of the main reasons remissioning begins with the life of the leader, exegeting culture and church, and identifying ruts we are stuck in is we must intentionally seek to know the places, people, stories, structures, and names within our church and community before we can truly understand the root issues of sin that need to be "gospeled."

When I moved to Ashland, Virginia, which literally uses as its slogan "the center of the universe," I noticed one of the ways this was true—no one ever told me their phone number with the area code. I had moved to this rural suburb from Northern Virginia, and this cultural marker let me know my new home saw itself as the center of culture and the world. In Northern Virginia, you always gave your area code because, one, there were many different area codes in that region, two, people moved in and out of the area often, bringing their existing phone numbers with them, and three, there was no "center" that everyone had to adjust to. In Richmond there were literally "come-here's" and "been-here's." Area codes were one way to quickly identify who wasn't a true native of the region.

The past always informs the present. To be able to navigate cultural complexities in the remissioning process, you must be willing to take a hard look at how your church and community became the places they are today. In the Richmond region there is a helpful book written by an Episcopal priest called *Richmond's Unhealed History* that functions as a historical examination of how race and class issues have created the modern situation we are in today.[3] How might you look back so you can live differently going forward? Take a look at the cultural and church exegesis work you have done and bring a different aim to the exercise this time. Look at how class and race inform the rituals, hopes, dreams, fears, and habits your church and community hold as meaningful. Where are the gaps between the vision of the kingdom laid out in Acts and Revelation and where you are at today?

Looking back in order to live forward is a learning phase. The more diverse your conversations, reading, listening, and learning are, the greater the chance you can move into other phases of the remissioning process with more thoughtful care and attention to creative destruction. Before jumping to any conclusions that you and your church "know what to do," especially in majority-white contexts, take some time to listen and learn. Where are the places your church or community has a short memory? Where are the places your church or community should be careful not to forget what has come before?

Two important theologies that must move from rarely practiced to the center of our habits are confession and repentance. Often our churches want to jump into healing, but it is essential that we take time to confess and repent first. James Cone points out, "There is no repentance without obedience and there is no obedience without action."[4] To repent is both to grow beyond our current way of seeing the world and to put that growth into action. Faith plus works!

To confess means we are willing to name and acknowledge the places our churches have gone astray and lifted up as central something that has diminished the kingdom view of Jesus. A couple of months before Martin Luther King Jr. was killed, he preached a message called "The Drum Major Instinct" where he named the way class diminished the message of the gospel because churches acted in ways that were indistinguishable from social clubs, fraternities, and other exclusive groups. Listen to this:

> I've been to churches you know, and they say, "We have so many doctors and so many schoolteachers, and many lawyers, and so many businessmen in our church." And that's fine, because doctors need to go to church, and lawyers, and businessmen, teachers—they ought to be in church. But they say that, even the preacher will sometime go on through it, they say that as if the other people don't count. And the church is the one place where a doctor ought to forget that he's a doctor. The church is the one place where a Ph.D. ought to forget that he's a Ph.D. The church is the one place that a schoolteacher ought to forget the degree she has behind her name. The church is the one place where the lawyer ought to forget that he's a lawyer. And any church that violates the "whosoever will, let him come" doctrine is a dead, cold church, and nothing but a little social club with a thin veneer of religiosity.[5]

Whew. That one stings a bit. None of us wants to be a social club with a thin veneer of religiosity, but to grow out of that way of being church requires the courage to confess the ways you have individually and collectively missed the mark of God's hopes for your kingdom citizenship. Can you be honest about the way race and class work in your context? Can you begin to name the way those sins work in your own heart as a leader? Can you demonstrate confession and repentance (name the sin, name how you want to grow beyond it, and then follow through in action) with those in your different spaces of belonging?

As Ken Wytsma points out in his book *The Myth of Equality*, "We don't want anything or anyone disrupting or subverting the religious climate that allows us to get along by not talking about things we find challenging or that confront our value system. If we did, those in economic, political, or religious power would suddenly feel like their control was slipping away. But by avoiding these difficult and uncomfortable issues, we reinforce privilege."[6]

As with all of remissioning, leading people to confession and repentance in these areas takes thoughtful exegesis and pacing. But to seek remissioning without acknowledging how race and class have impacted our churches and caused them to lose their sense of mission is to try to treat symptoms without addressing root causes.

Ultimately, remissioning has always been aimed at helping churches wake up to the mission of God. It's a process of taking the natural order of ways you are church, journeying with your people through a process of disorder, then inviting them to join in the work of the Spirit that is reordering the church and community into citizenship in the kingdom of God. Confessing and repenting of sin have never been fun parts of Christianity or following Jesus. But they are important gifts that come to us through Christ, where grace gets the final word and relationships that seem beyond repair can be restored through the love of God.

Churches are people collectively living into a story together. Remissioning our established churches asks what story we want to inhabit with each other as we follow Jesus. Will we take time to ask how our worship, programs, leadership, budget, staffing, and formation groups are helping us live into the diversity of God's kingdom? Where are the entry points for people of different cultures and economic situations? Are there places of leadership for diverse people in our contexts? Could our churches be intentional to learn from other churches in the community, building friendships and sitting under the leadership of people who have a different cultural norm than ours? As leaders, do we regularly put ourselves in situations where we can model the kind of relationships we want to see in our church?

Personal Journey

It started with friendship. Pastor Randell Williams of Shiloh Baptist Church in my town became my friend. We shared meals. Our families gathered together. We navigated the loss of a child. We were both young pastors remissioning our churches but from very different contexts. I am a white man pastoring a historically white church. Randell is an African American pastoring a historically Black church. And our relationship changed us. Most importantly, out of deep friendship our churches are remissioning together.

In 2016 David Bailey, a public theologian and catalyst for reconciling communities, was the first person of color to preach in my church—and some people stood up and walked out as he entered the pulpit. Majority-white churches like my own that have held a relatively moderate place in our denominational context (ordaining and calling women in ministry and leadership for over sixty years) most often think sexuality will be the most divisive issue they will face. However, because of their lack of proximity to diverse relationships, these churches experience the most conflict over race and ethnicity. What started in 2016 would heat up to a boil in the coming years as First Baptist Church Ashland grew in friendship with Shiloh.

In January of 2018, Pastor Randell invited our churches to worship together and for me to preach at his church. In our more than 150 years of existence only a couple of blocks apart from one another, our churches had never worshiped together. In a packed house our churches sang, prayed, and invited God's power to help us dream new dreams and have new hope for what it meant to be God's people in Ashland, Virginia. That night we asked God to help us not ignore the differences in the color of our skin and learn to bring our whole selves for the sake of a greater mission.

Pastor Randell and Shiloh Baptist have had the most to lose by choosing to be in relationship with my church. We are a First Baptist church, which in my denomination means wealthy, majority-white, and often run like a social club. Folks in my congregation held positions of leadership and power in our community, often the very positions of leadership and power denied to the people of Shiloh for years. People in my church were descendants of families who owned plantations, while the predecessors of Shiloh worked as slaves or servants. There were still people living from my church who'd hired people from Shiloh to work in their factories or clean their homes. The tension our congregations felt was born out of experiencing history from very different places of power. Our schools were marked by the challenges of integration and our county was known as a community of deep-seated racism. In 2020, the KKK from North Carolina sent a group of Klansmen to recruit new members just a few miles from both of our churches in front of our county courthouse.

Despite these structural and deep-seated marks of injustice, Shiloh welcomed us in as the stranger and sought relationships with us.

In the spring of 2019 our churches received a grant to "connect worship to life, bridging racial divides." We had been growing together and decided to take an intentional step to form learning communities that shared leadership, learned each other's stories, and wrote devotional guides that we could share in our community as ways to connect through faith.

However, before we could take any meaningful steps toward these goals, three different groups of people sought to remove me as pastor. Being awarded the grant was the final straw for those who had withheld their financial offerings in order to create pressure that might lead to a call for my removal. One group consisted of people who had previously held power and leadership in the church but had slowly been moved to the margins because of their difficulty maintaining emotional and spiritual equilibrium. Another group was made up of fundamentalists: those who said I was leading us too far and too fast—as well as those who said I was not going far or fast enough. And the final group consisted of those who simply didn't want to worship with people of a different race—they could have their church and we could have ours.

In moments like this on the remissioning journey, when the temperature is reaching a boil, it's tempting to overutilize the pulpit to force a change or crisis moment. I wanted to yell and scream and throw my hands up in disgust. But remissioning leaders must learn how to manage their own anxiety in Christ while not shying away from the pain these situations cause (and being careful not to heap the pain onto communities of color, who already have enough to navigate). These conversations require nuance, patience, and more than a monologue. But public and communal acts of sin also require communal repentance. So what does this look like?

During that summer of 2019 when some folks were trying to remove me as pastor, we had about two hundred conversations in various settings—individuals, small groups of two to eight, larger groups of ten or more. When the issues became clear, we shut off the livestream of our service, and only then did I name things from the pulpit and invite the church to a time of communal repentance and prayer.

At this point in our remissioning journey we believed ourselves to be in a similar place as the Israelites wandering in the wilderness. We had been freed from some of the deep brokenness and bondage of Egypt, but we were still in the wilderness and did not yet have the character we needed to live in the promised land. The wandering and grumbling were signs that if we did make it to the promised land, we might mistake it for something we had accomplished with our own effort instead of a gift of God's grace and provision.

On August 11, 2019, I asked people to consider what they were holding on to that might prohibit them from entering the promised land God had for us. Would they name the ways they had contributed to this moment in our church where we were considering alienating our sister church because of the color of their skin? I asked them to name specific ways they had contributed to racial and class inequity in our church and community, post these confessions on crosses in our sanctuary, and pray about them with staff and each other, asking God what it meant to be obedient through action. It was humbling to hear a ninety-five-year-old woman repent of her attitude on the desegregation of schools in our county and seek restoration with people in our church and her family. My friend Lori Ruffin reminds me regularly, "There is always room at the altar for confession and repentance."

After this incredible time of worship, confession, and repentance, we walked to our old chapel to have a business meeting where the church could allow its worship of God to inform a discussion about God's mission for our church. Church leaders led the people courageously to discuss what God was asking us to live into as followers of Jesus. We invited all the folks who were angry, frustrated, and disappointed in the ways we had been remissioning over the previous four years and upset with my leadership and the staff.

In that room the Spirit moved, and the people talked and disagreed and confronted each other in love. And the leaders helped our church recognize that in this moment the vote was not about staffing—the vote was about our mission: "First Baptist Church Ashland will continue to make disciples who love Jesus and love their neighbors through unity, hospitality, and neighboring and we affirm the direction of our church to lay down our individual preferences for the sake of God's mission in our community and beyond." We would not let someone's race or ethnicity determine our willingness to love.

In that business meeting the church unanimously voted to walk forward together. And from the floor of that same meeting a vote was called to affirm the current staff who had led the church to that crisis point so we could understand this moment as a place of breakthrough and rejection of the back-to-Egypt committee's pressure to resume bondage. The church affirmed unanimously that the current staff and I were leading us in precisely the direction we needed to go to love our neighbors well.

After so much heartache and pain, we were able to put the worship grant into practice. We are learning in this remissioning journey, through the gift of Shiloh's patience, prayer, and friendship, that proximity and presence in relationships help us worship God more fully and see the image of God in each other. We learned that when we take our differences seriously, we can find unity on the other side through friendship. The work for racial justice through regular emphasis is essential for our formation.

In the summer of 2020, Shiloh and First Baptist helped gather faith leaders to lead a march of prayer and song from the center of town to Shiloh's campus while working with local police to talk about how to create a safe community together. Our churches are called on by social services to help support families when violence has led to the death of a child.

In 2023 our churches started a nonprofit together called Empowering Neighbors that pursues thriving communities. When one of the small business owners in our church exegeted our town, they realized that median-income households qualified for free tax services through a federal grant program. So our first program is helping provide tax services. It is housed at Shiloh and is partnering with town, businesses, and neighborhoods to serve families.

My church has transitioned in the last four years from a place resistant to loving its neighbors who are a different race or ethnicity to running an English Speakers of Other Languages program, sponsoring an Afghan family for humanitarian parole, welcoming Muslim families worshiping with us as they make a new home in our community and seek to learn about Jesus, and becoming a signpost in our community of how the gospel can transform people's lives.

This is one way a church can remission from the inside out.

MAKING AND TAKING NEXT STEPS

The disruptive work necessary to wake up many churches to issues of race and class will not happen overnight, but it can happen. This work will require a lot of you as a leader and as a church. And it most likely will cost you some people. I encourage you to find another leader or church that is going through this process and ask if you can pray for one another, learn from each other, and have someone to lean on when the road gets tough. Having friends and guides along the way is important. Please don't rush to the end and try to skip the confession and repentance part of the journey. It always backfires, and it leads to mistrust when those who have benefited from the way things are never come to understand they are part of the problem.

As a leader, be sure to take time to stay close to Christ. Ask a few friends to pray with you and for you regularly. And know that deep down you are following the cross-laden path of Christ and the saints who have gone before you.

Practically, here are some suggestions to take some next steps:

- Use Table 16.1, Navigating race, class, and the kingdom of God, and Table 16.2, Remissioning exegesis, at the end of this chapter, to reflect on the multiple cultures present in your community and church. Use the framing questions with Table 16.2 to gain perspective on how your community and church may have new things to learn, places of brokenness to repent of, and opportunities to practice justice and reconciliation.

- Seek out relationships with leaders from churches that have different cultural expressions from your church. Seek ways to learn from how they follow Jesus. Can you fill out an exegesis chart with them about their faith community? What would it look like to begin bridge-building with one another toward each other?

- Consider what it would look like to have meals, host leadership gatherings, and spend more time in places you were blind to prior to receiving new eyes to see. How might you support local businesses, other churches, other nonprofits, or community leaders who are trying to create a thicker net for relationships?

- Many people want to focus on learning but don't take tangible steps to grow relationally. As you learn, think about how you can take meaningful steps to mature your understanding of race, class, and the kingdom of God in your church while also improving the proximity and presence of your church to real people.

It is critically important to approach crosscultural work in remissioning without a savior complex. Remember that remissioning relies on receiving this work as a gift to steward rather than coming to others as though you have all the answers. Before coming up with a plan to "change your community"—listen to your community. Invite their voices and the way God's image is alive in them to shape your imagination for how beautifully God's kingdom breakthrough can be.

Further Reading

Martin Luther King Jr., *A Testament of Hope: The Essential Writings and Speeches of Martin Luther King Jr.*, ed. James M. Washington (New York: HarperCollins, 1991).

Mark Charles and Soong-Chan Rah, *Unsettling Truths: The Ongoing, Dehumanizing Legacy of the Doctrine of Discovery* (Downers Grove, IL: InterVarsity Press, 2019).

Latasha Morrison, *Be the Bridge: Pursuing God's Heart for Racial Reconciliation* (Colorado Springs, CO: Waterbrook, 2019).

Ken Wytsma, *The Myth of Equality: Uncovering the Roots of Injustice and Privilege* (Downers Grove, IL: InterVarsity Press, 2017).

Richard Rothstein, *The Color of Law: A Forgotten History of How Our Government Segregated America* (New York: Liveright, 2017).

Jemar Tisby, *The Color of Compromise: The Truth about the American Church's Complicity in Racism* (Grand Rapids, MI: Zondervan, 2020).

James Cone, *Black Theology & Black Power* (Maryknoll, NY: Orbis, 2006).

Jonathan Wilson-Hartgrove, *Reconstructing the Gospel: Finding Freedom from Slave-holder Religion* (Downers Grove, IL: InterVarsity Press, 2018).

Benjamin Campbell, *Richmond's Unhealed History* (Richmond, VA: Brandyland, 2011).

Lisa Sharon Harper, *The Very Good Gospel: How Everything Wrong Can Be Made Right* (Colorado Springs, CO: Waterbrook 2016).

Soong-Chan Rah, *The Next Evangelicalism: Freeing the Church from Western Cultural Captivity* (Downers Grove, IL: InterVarsity Press, 2009).

Table 16.1. Navigating race, class, and the kingdom of God

Cultural component	Examples	Implication
Places		
Rituals		
Practices		
Values		
Dreams		
Fears		
Language		

FRAMING QUESTIONS:

- Where can my church pay attention to and learn from cultures other than our own?
- How are each of these cultural components informed by race, class, and where the kingdom is breaking in?

Table 16.2. Remissioning exegesis

Cultural component	Question	Examples	Implication
Places	Where do people gather, spend time, and relate to one another for formation, play, and relationships?	Local coffee shops, restaurants, concert venues, bars, parks, historical sites, etc.	These places serve as part of the public imagination and as locations where people gather.
Rituals	What repeatable events, programs, and ceremonies does your community participate in together?	Parades, fairs, special holidays, school functions, and seasonal activities that have historical or traditional roots, etc.	These events and programs give rhythm to how people gather and are born out of history or tradition.
Practices	How does your community act together as a community through work, play, conflict, and relationships?	Parades, fairs, special holidays, school functions, and seasonal activities that are future oriented for what the community desires to become, etc.	These events or programs give rhythm to how people gather and are birthing new life in the community.
Values	What does your community hold as important, name as being of worth, and lift up as good?	Freedom, care for the earth, care for others, collaboration, innovation, hope, being business friendly, etc.	These values guide the way people relate and support the way you faithfully live into the community.
Dreams	What does your community hope it will become in the years ahead?	What story or stories do people tell when they describe the community flourishing in the years to come? Welcoming to new families; having great schools, thriving businesses, great art, etc.	These dreams help give an orientation for what success and flourishing look like in their mind's eye.
Fears	What or who does your community fear?	What story or stories do people tell when they describe what they hope will not happen in the years to come? Having no children or young families; closing businesses, struggling schools, a lack of diversity, etc.	These fears help give an orientation for what failure and disappointment look like in their mind's eye.
Language	How does your community communicate with one another?	Digital, social media, apps, print, storefronts, mailings, etc.	Communication tells you about how people think, live, work, and play in your community.

PART FIVE

REMISSIONING LEADERSHIP

There needs to be not only the awareness of overt racism but also
of covert privilege. Are we asking the questions: "Who do we
gravitate toward?" "Who do we favor?" and "Who benefits?"

SOONG-CHAN RAH, THE NEXT EVANGELICALISM

Lead us up beyond unknowing and light,
Up to the farthest, highest peak
Of mystic scripture,
Where the mysteries of God's Word
Lie simple, absolute and unchangeable
In the brilliant darkness of hidden silence.

PSEUDO-DIONYSIUS, THE COMPLETE WORKS

Everything we do, think, feel, imagine, discuss is framed by
the notion of whether our death is the end or the beginning
of something else. It takes great faith to have no faith.

BONO, SURRENDER

17

HABITS + VISION = REMISSIONING

Incremental daily progress (negative or positive) is what actually causes transformation. A figurative drip, drip, drip. Showing up, every single day, gaining in strength, organizing for the long haul, building connection, laying track—this subtle but difficult work is how culture changes. . . . If you want to cause action in the short run, the opposite is true. In the short run, drip by drip rarely puts people on alert. It's the thunderclap, the coordinated, accelerating work of many people, that causes those in power to sit up and take notice.

SETH GODIN, "DRIP BY DRIP AND THE THUNDERCLAP"

ONE OF THE MOST DIFFICULT CHALLENGES of remissioning is resisting the urge to speed up or introduce novelty when what is most appropriate is slow, steady work in the same direction.

Seth Godin, the branding and marketing guru, helps us understand this in his drip, drip, drip and thunderclap imagery above. Remissioning is most often a drip, drip, drip process, happening a little bit at a time, with thunderclap moments less common, especially in the early years. Throughout this book we've focused on bite-sized pieces that help us remission in everyday activities like meetings, discipleship, pruning, and community exegesis. Breaking remissioning into parts and steadily asking questions that help us see who our neighbors are and where our churches are headed can help us adapt and transform. Divine experiments and skunkworks help provide thunderclap opportunities of more dramatic change, but early thunderclaps must be thoughtfully strategic.

Systems don't change with the wave of a magic wand, and to see established churches transformed we need generous, humble-hearted leaders who will press into the slow work of steady change. While I am supportive of church plants, I don't think that any new work begins with a blank slate. Instead, we start new churches with people who hold unexamined assumptions about how life works, and if we aren't careful we will continue to propagate an evangelicalism that is captive to Western (and often white Western) worldviews, habits, and shared practices.[1]

Doctors, police officers, and pilots become proficient at their jobs when they have completed vast amounts of training. There is a reason it takes months upon months, years upon years, to be prepared for certain professions. When crisis strikes, an unexpected situation arises, or emotions become elevated, you don't want a doctor, police officer, or pilot who freezes in the moment. You want someone who can withstand the pressure and use their habits to navigate the situation with skill and wisdom.

Many established churches and their leaders feel like they're in a pressure cooker, without the training and habits to navigate a changing environment. When people feel the pressure rising, emotions heat up, often leading to thunderclap moments of decline.

This is why our habits matter. We can have big ideas about God, about what it means to be church and how we can be on mission with God, but without the habits to put that theology into practice, how do we expect transformation to take place? There are no easy buttons.

ADAPTIVE CAPACITY

One of the core competencies remissioning churches must develop is that of adaptive leadership, a concept pioneered by Ronald Heifetz and Marty Linsky and explored further by Tod Bolsinger, who writes:

> *Adaptive leadership* is not about finding the best-known or most-available fix to a problem, but instead adapting to the changing environment or circumstances so that new possibilities arise for accurately *seeing, understanding,* and *facing* challenges with *new actions.* Just as an organism must

adapt in order to thrive in a changing environment, so organizations need to adapt to the changing world around them without losing their core identity, their reason for being, their core values and purpose. This kind of leadership is complex and fraught with loss, fears, and anxiety, causing us to feel off-balance and insecure. But it is the essence of leadership in a changing world.[2]

To develop new habits, we need a new mindset. Adaptive leadership is a way to think about the role of pastor and leader in a new context with an expanded purpose. You are not the whack-a-mole pastor who tackles every new problem that comes their way without organizational self-awareness or discernment about what needs attention and direction.

According to Heifetz and Linsky, "Leadership is disturbing people at a rate they can absorb."[3] Another way of phrasing this is: remissioning leadership is disappointing people at a rate they can absorb and continue on in the process with you. Adaptive leadership is recognizing that transformation requires loss (what we've called creative destruction) and this kind of leadership requires you to lead in new ways. It requires growth in self-awareness and a depersonalization of the way people express frustration with your leadership. Learning to differentiate between what is yours to carry and what is not is a lifelong learning process, but with new habits those muscles can grow and help you become an adaptive leader.

The capacity to navigate change depends on growing our adaptive abilities. Heifetz and Linsky write, "Habits, values, and attitudes, even dysfunctional ones, are part of one's identity. To change the way people see and do things is to challenge how they define themselves."[4] Your own habits as a leader are directly related to your church's capacity to navigate the losses related to change and to adapt to God's invitation to mission for the sake of your neighbors. Your habits (how you spend your time and the practices that shape your life) inform how your church perceives your leadership and understands what you value.

In many established churches we focus on thunderclap moments and fool ourselves into thinking big, out-of-the-ordinary attendance numbers on Easter or Christmas or heavy consumer experiences in our programs demonstrate "success" or fruitfulness. What would it look like to measure how often we disappoint people for not creating a church that made them comfortable or required no transformation? What would it look like to walk regularly into the loss people express without fixing it for them? How might those habits help our churches grow in their adaptive capacity?

REMISSIONING HABITS

Adaptive leadership for established churches that are trying to remission requires new habits. While not exhaustive, this list of new habits is informed by the big story of the Scriptures and can help you put positive practices into place, developing new metrics of fruitfulness. How can your church drip, drip, drip these habits in your everyday practices?

Unity. Remissioned churches look for ways to grow in unity for the sake of a larger mission. Unity is not uniformity or an ignorance of difference. Unity is a willingness to pursue a mission together because of our differences and in celebration of differences. There is a kind of cheap unity that seeks to obliterate and ignore differences where everyone will conform to a majority culture or nostalgic way of being church. This is not the kind of unity remissioning churches practice. That is assimilation.

When Paul talks about unity and diversity in the body of Christ, he explains how all of the parts are necessary and exist to further the mission together (1 Cor 12:12-30). Established churches often elevate preferences over willingness to sacrifice for unity in the body. Unity is a commitment to stay as connected as possible, pursuing forgiveness, reconciliation, and seeing each other as made in the image of God. What habits can help your church grow unity?

Hospitality. Hospitality is imagining what it might be like to walk in someone else's shoes—to see and hear the world from someone else's perspective. This is a critical habit for remissioning churches and is connected to practicing the regular exegesis of our community and church. Hospitality helps you appreciate diversity as a gift from God and navigate conversations on race, culture, theological differences, sexuality, politics, generational differences, and much more. It helps your church see the world from other people's perspectives instead of assuming everyone sees it from the same perspective either inside or outside your church.

When your church learns to practice hospitality in everyday life, how might this change the tone of business decisions? How might hospitality inform the way staff relate to each other and grow in self-awareness? Could the regular practice of hospitality provide opportunities to grow in adaptive leadership? How does a practice of hospitality help you think about who benefits and who is left out of your church's mission, programming, and *telos*?

Abundance. "Now to him who is able to do immeasurably more than all we ask or imagine, according to his power that is at work within us, to him be glory in the church and in Christ Jesus throughout all generations, forever and ever! Amen" (Eph 3:20-21). What habits would you put in place if you and your leadership believed this was God's hope for your church? I'm not talking about a get-big-quick scheme, but rather the regular habit of believing that God desires good for your church not only for its own sake but for the sake of generations to come. How would you live out the hope of God for your church empowered by the imagination and power of God? Remissioning churches live out of a sense of God's abundance rather than the fear of scarcity. Scarcity leads to survival, whereas abundance contributes to fruitfulness.

How can your church regularly trust in God's provision and adopt an abundance mindset rather than living in constant fear that there will never be enough? Instead of focusing on loss when a majority culture must decrease so others might increase, how might our hope in the abundance of God diminish fear, make room for confession and repentance, and see that in the economy of God, five loaves and two fish are more than enough? What if there is enough grace for healing in relationships? What if there are enough people in your community for all of the churches to thrive instead of being in competition? How might your church regularly practice abundance instead of scarcity?

Shift from consumer to citizen. Many of the habits necessary to remission a church are based in this shift from creating consumers of religious goods and services to developing active participants who are citizens of the kingdom of God. What does participation look like in your context? Is it easier for folks to consume religious activities than share in leadership? How do your worship, meetings, meals, and other practices invite people to take up stewardship in the life of your church? Is there both an invitation to serve and a challenge to serve inside and outside your church?

The shift from consumer to citizen is based on the theological conviction that every person is made in the image of God and can bring themselves, their vulnerabilities, and their abilities to contribute to the mission of God. What would it look like to practice this shift from consumer to citizen in the way you navigate conflict? The way you make teams and committees? The way you see people who are vulnerable or marginalized because of their abilities, socioeconomic background, or lack of church experience? How do you invite people of different abilities to lead, bring their gifts, and have places of honor in your church?

What other habits could you develop to inform who you are becoming as a church? Our everyday drip, drip, drip habits shape who we are becoming and have already shaped who you are now. Adaptive leadership is developing new habits that in the long term provide opportunities to navigate loss and explore a new future.

All of the things your church does on Sundays, Wednesdays, in small groups, on mission pathways, during committee meetings, and in every facet of life inform how you are being the church for the sake of the world Jesus came to love, serve, and be resurrected for. Paying attention to our shared habits and growing our capacity to change is how we help our churches navigate losses and experience remissioning in everyday life.

When my church in Ashland was navigating the shift from two preference-based worship services to one unified service, we named the ways our preferences had inhibited our ability to be unified, diminished our ability to practice hospitality, grown a culture of competition, and kept people stuck consuming worship instead of participating in it. A few weeks after the church decided to permanently stay with one worship service so we could disciple one another into a new way of being church, a church member called to voice her sense of loss.

It was courageous of Martha to call. She described how her ability to read music, sing complex songs, and appreciate the beauty of the old hymns felt muddled with the new songs and repetitive choruses. Martha loved knowing what to expect each week in the service order and how to participate in the pieces she already knew and understood.

When I asked her why those songs, the steadiness of the traditions, and the predictable worship were so important to her, she told me how her husband had died and an adult child and grandchild had moved in with her. The changes she faced in her everyday life were too much. Martha liked worshiping in a way that made her feel safe, comfortable, and grounded. It was a gracious and kind phone call. She wasn't angry. She was naming profound loss in her life and explaining how worship provided comfort amid those open wounds.

I apologized to Martha.

"I'm so sorry," I said. "Our church failed you. We didn't help you grow the muscles needed to navigate change and make sense of the losses you've had to walk through. We fooled you and ourselves into thinking our best work is keeping everything the same. We didn't help you know that God walks through the hardest parts of life with us when we feel alone. We could have been helping you grieve and welcome your child home with inner strength. I'm sorry we let you down all these years. We'd love the opportunity to grow with you as you go through these hardships and help you know God is with you. But I also understand that this might feel like too much change at once to have the ability to stay. We love you and care for you, and on behalf of your church I'm sorry we didn't equip you as we should have by learning how to grow through change together."

We grow mature disciples who can confess and repent of racism by leading through it with new habits.

We grow mature disciples who can lay down their preferences for a bigger mission by leading through it with new habits.

We grow mature disciples who can honor the past without worshiping it by leading through it with new habits.

We grow mature disciples who can experience loss and practice resurrection by leading through it with new habits.

Habits in connection with a *telos* vision worth dying for and then living for is how remissioning truly happens.

Further Reading

Samuel Wells, *Improvisation: The Drama of Christian Ethics* (Grand Rapids, MI: Brazos, 2004).

Ronald Heifetz and Marty Linsky, *Leadership on the Line: Staying Alive through the Dangers of Leading* (Boston: Harvard Business School Press, 2017).

John McKnight and Peter Block, *The Abundant Community: Awakening the Power of Families and Neighborhoods* (San Francisco: Berrett-Koehler, 2010).

18

EMBRACING CONFLICT AS REMISSIONING LEADERS

*That grievance story, more than what hurt you, has
imprisoned you. It keeps you in the past.*

FRED LUSKIN, *FORGIVE FOR GOOD*

*When a person is at their most oppositional, that is the time when they
are most vulnerable. Instead of ignoring or attempting to overwhelm
this resistance, we are free to see it as our ally, by not responding the
way we normally would.*

JAMES OSTERHAUS, JOSEPH JURKOWSKI, AND TODD HAHN,
THRIVING THROUGH MINISTRY CONFLICT

IN THE GREAT OUTDOORS it is not uncommon to see a tree that is
leaning to the side or whose trunk is twisted. On mountainsides it's common
for all trees to bend in the same way based on the direction of the wind or
erosion of the soil.[1]

In Oracle, Arizona, a biodome was created as a center for learning how
plants and ecosystems fare in a closed ecological system (see biosphere2
.org). Constructed in the late 1980s, its leadership shifted from independent scientists to Columbia University and now the University of Arizona.[2] One of its discoveries was that trees grew incredibly fast, and many

bent unusually. The controlled environment of the biodome created conditions for rapid growth, diminished stress, and increased height. The biodome was a near-perfect environment for the trees. But their quick growth and lack of stress caused them to be "etoliated," which means they were taller and thinner than trees outside the dome. Mark Nelson, one of the original scientists in the experiment, explained, "This particularly affected trees, which also lacked 'stress wood,' higher strength tissue produced with exposure to high turbulence winds. This led to some drooping of trees."[3]

The trees needed stress to get stronger. The lack of wind and other external pressures created unsustainable growth. In other words, a distressed tree is better than a perfect tree. When a tree faces environmental pressures, it matures with greater stability and grows more sustainably toward sunlight. Distressed trees are less likely to snap over time.

It may be tempting to avoid the stresses that develop in your church and within your own soul as you lead through the remissioning process. But what if the maturity you need to become strong, healthy, and sustainable is undercut when you avoid conflict?

Don't Bail

Conflict isn't fun, but it isn't a bad thing for you or your church. I once had someone who disliked our new worship music and thought I downloaded sermons from the internet (because I used my iPad to preach) ask if he could host a watch party for another church's service on Sunday mornings—on our campus. I wish I had asked if he was going to take up an offering with this group, but instead I just said no. And then I asked Rob a few more questions. If he wanted to be involved in this church via television, should I call that pastor in the event Rob needed a hospital visit or support through a difficult situation in his life? Rob paused for a moment and realized that he hadn't considered those details and backed off the request. Rob would eventually leave the church, but it was a transition filled with grace and prayer, and years later when my family experienced a financial challenge, Rob became aware and sent support.

When conflict happens, many church leaders shut down or take it as a sign that they've led poorly. Sometimes we do lead poorly, but sometimes when unspoken or unrealistic expectations come to the surface, conflict is productive.

The first session in every premarriage coaching series I lead for couples includes this question: Do you know how to fight well with each other? There is no joy in asking or answering this question, but their answers or non-answers tell me a lot. When a newly-in-love couple tells me they don't really fight because they love each other so much, it tells me they need time to mature together. When a couple says they fight just fine because the other person always wins, it tells me they have issues listening and voicing their perspectives to one another. When a couple says they fight often but rarely reach resolution, it tells me they understand the need for conflict but would benefit from tools and habits to help them navigate their pain in a meaningful way.

Tod Bolsinger highlights what's at stake for leaders in their experience of conflict:

> The real challenge of leadership is not tactical or strategic but *emotional*. Not only do we have to deal with the inner uncertainty that goes with leading into uncharted territory, but we also have to manage the two-front battle, which includes our own need to be liked, to gain approval from others or to be seen as a competent professional. And sometimes we get really anxious that we are never going to measure up.[4]

I think we all know in our gut that Bolsinger is right. Conflict often goes right to the core of our emotional life as leaders.

The temptation in conflict is to gravitate to one of four behaviors: survive, control, accept/avoid, or perform. In survival mode we do what is necessary to make it through. In survival mode we may not win but we most certainly will not lose. Survival is about making it out alive, come hell or high water. Control in conflict demonstrates that we have power and the other person does not. In control mode we do whatever it takes to secure our own emotional borders.

The third temptation in emotional conflict is to accept blame too readily or avoid blame altogether (even if that means not assigning it to the person we are in conflict with). Acceptance and avoidance are two sides of the same emotional coin that keep conflict at a distance. The last temptation in conflict is to perform, in other words, to demonstrate competence in the issue at hand without addressing the emotional space it has opened in the relationship. In this temptation the aim is to demonstrate superiority with no change in behavior.

Here's what these temptations reveal: when conflict arises, we have an array of defense mechanisms that keep us stuck in immaturity instead of embracing conflict as a means for transformation. I had a coach once tell me that our defense mechanisms are not to fool other people; they are to fool ourselves so we don't have to change or deal with the issues before us (see http://drdanelash.com). Which is a way of pointing out that in conflict we really learn the most about ourselves.

This means it's important for a leader to stay in conflict and grow in awareness of the temptation to avoid it. If you learn to do this well, you might also discover how your church avoids conflict. The more aware you are of those tendencies, the better you and your church can navigate conflict together. The most important thing is not to avoid it but be willing to stay in it.

THE NATURE OF CONFLICT

Thriving Through Ministry Conflict is a book that offers some perspective on the nature of conflict in churches and how our temptation to avoid it is counterproductive to the changes we hope to see. The authors describe conflict like this:

> 1. Conflict is inescapable. Because of the major differences between human beings, it is a wonder there actually is not more conflict than we already experience.
>
> 2. The problem is not conflict itself but how people relate to one another when they are in conflict.
>
> 3. Conflict is both good and necessary because it elicits different points of view, clears the air, and makes it possible to resolve extraordinarily complex issues.[5]

Many churches and leaders think of conflict as a sign that things are wrong, broken, and in danger of shutting down. To remission a church requires learning to navigate conflict with intention and recognizing that conflict is a sign of cultural values clashing—and an indication that real transformation is on the horizon. Adaptive leaders in remissioning churches learn to see conflict as their friend, not in some sadistic or proud way, but viewing conflict as a tutor that reveals what is at stake culturally as you navigate into a healthy future.

At the root of conflict are behaviors that reveal differences in mission, vision, and values. Edwin Friedman is right when he says we can't think our way out of the gridlock that comes with conflict and remissioning. He writes, "Conceptually stuck systems cannot become unstuck simply by trying harder."[6] Instead, we need new habits that reshape how we make disciples.

If we shouldn't and can't avoid conflict, we need new ways to relate to each other in conflict and to remember it is a magnifying glass that helps us see the competing values at stake in our churches. So how do we embrace conflict in the process of remissioning our churches?

FIGHTING WELL

The premise of this chapter is that conflict can be a teacher that helps churches remission and experience internal transformation to become better neighbors. What if churches became the training ground for healthy conflict navigation so that reconciliation and transformation could take place in our communities, marriages, families, and places of work and play? This is what is at stake. The church is meant to be the formation school of a particular people who demonstrate through our shared lives that Jesus' rule and reign is present on earth as in heaven.

Here are a couple of practical tips to help you navigate and embrace conflict with intention and create the possibility of transformation (first within yourself and then within your church).

Focus on behaviors. People say all kinds of things about what they value. They say it in scathing emails. They say it in awkward business meetings. They say it in the hallway behind your back. But you can know what someone truly believes not by what they say but by how they act. In conflict, the important thing to pay attention to is behavior and actions. How are you acting toward someone else? Have your actions demonstrated integrity around the values you are discussing? What has the person you are in conflict with demonstrated with their actions? By focusing on behaviors we learn to push through rhetoric and see people for who they are instead of who they say they are. Focus on behaviors and the habits that make transformation possible.

Instead of endlessly debating ideas, discern how the ideas impact the way people live. How do our actions shape our relationships, our mission, our way of being church? What do our actions reveal about what is important to us?

Regulate the temperature. Bolsinger says leadership is like a slow cooker: slow, steady heat that produces a great meal. If the temperature is too low, you won't cook the food and it won't become edible. If the temperature is too high, you'll burn it up and have nothing to eat. A leader's job is to regulate the temperature of the organization. And the best way to do that is by regulating urgency and anxiety. Urgency is when you need to move fast and the issue before you is ripe for action. But urgency should be used carefully, because if every issue that comes your church's way is urgent, then nothing is urgent. In terms of anxiety, your job as a leader is to be the least anxious presence in the room. Often people want to make something urgent when more time, perspective, or wisdom is needed. When they feel anxious to *do something right now!,* your job is to regulate that anxiety.[7]

Does your leadership regulate the temperature or does it raise it so high it burns everything up? Who else in your church regulates the temperature? How can you set expectations and rules for meetings so your conflict can be productive and not destructive? How might your preparation for a meeting help mediate anxiety? Are you a slow cooker or a microwave in times of conflict?

Ask good questions and listen well. Once during a church business meeting an attendee was frustrated about a candidate we had recommended hiring. This attendee came to the meeting prepared with a ten-minute speech chronicling why the candidate wasn't a good fit. It felt like they'd brought a bazooka to a knife fight. After the diatribe ended, I calmly thanked this attendee for their comments and asked which concern they wanted me to address first. I refused to respond with equal heat and force, which defused the situation and allowed the rest of the people in the meeting to make a wise decision without anxiety. The church leadership took a similar approach to worship conflict. They listened to the frustrations people named and instead of taking them personally, they asked good questions and reflected back what they heard. These skills have been especially helpful in business meetings, town halls, and feedback sessions.

If you find yourself becoming frustrated, take the time to listen as well as you can and ask good questions about what the other person is saying. Work your way toward the "why" questions that get at the heart of motivation and desire. It is impossible to ask good questions without listening well, seeking to understand a person before being understood yourself. In doing this during conflict you are demonstrating hospitality that is consistent with following Jesus.

Honor boundaries. One of the biggest challenges for leaders in embracing conflict is honoring boundaries, first for yourself and then for the person you are in conflict with. Friedman sums it up well: "The twin problems confronting leadership in our society today, the failure of nerve and the desire for a quick fix, are not the result of overly strong self but of weak or no self."[8] In the conversations about defense mechanisms above, that same coach told me our defense mechanisms trick us into believing a lie about what we are capable of or how we should handle a situation. Honoring our boundaries is about creating space to recognize that we get things wrong, we are finite creatures, we can't change other people, we can't keep sabotage from happening, and our own emotional health impacts how we lead. If you don't practice sabbath, find time to rest, and honor your own boundaries, how do you expect those who follow you to do the same?

Invite people to the balcony. From the proverbial balcony of your organization, you have a much wider view of what is possible and where gridlock is occurring. What might it look like for you to invite some leaders to see your church from a larger perspective so they might grow in their understanding of the big picture? From the larger vantage point you are able to see how the pieces and parts work together as a whole. When is the last time you brought your leadership community into a space to think creatively about why you do what you do? Conflict often looks different when you are outside of it. Looking at challenging relationships from a broader perspective can help regulate the temperature and put the puzzle pieces in place.

Forgive for good. In times of conflict we often conflate the grievance story out of our frustration that something hasn't worked out the way we planned. Fred Luskin says, "The grievance story is our tale of helplessness and frustration based on taking something too personally and blaming someone else for how we feel."[9] The longer we remain stuck in the grievance story of perceived wrong, the more challenging it is to let go of conflict and choose health.

Learning to forgive is what it means to live out the uncomfortable parts of the Scriptures, like loving our enemies and going with the soldier the extra mile. Forgiveness is an essential part of remissioning because it keeps our hearts soft in the middle of so much conflict and hurriedness.

Embracing conflict is an essential part of the remissioning journey, and it helps you navigate toward the future without ignoring the discomfort produced by clashing cultural values. What conflict are you avoiding right now that is removing focus on what is next for your church?

Years later when Rob, the gentleman who wanted us to have watch parties for other church services during our worship time, finally was ready to leave the church, we met together. We both named some of the disagreements we'd had, but we did it with kindness and contrite hearts, and we wished things could have been different. I prayed for Rob as he moved to a new church home and asked him to pray for me and our church as he left. We shook hands, exchanged emails from time to time, and were kind to one another when we saw each other at funerals.

A few years later, through some family challenges, we got custody of my nieces and nephew for a couple of years. One of the first cards I received in the mail was from Rob. He described for the first time where some of his childhood pain had come from and how he, too, had to live with his aunt and uncle for a season. Inside the card were a couple of hundred-dollar bills to take the kids somewhere fun—and a commitment to pray for my family.

Forgiveness helps the seeds of grace to grow in our remissioning churches. Boiling anger and endless complaints choke those seeds before they can grow and bear fruit.

FURTHER READING

Fred Luskin, *Forgive for Good: A Proven Prescription for Health and Happiness* (New York: HarperSanFrancisco, 2002).

James P. Osterhaus, Joseph M. Jurkowski, and Todd A. Hahn, *Thriving Through Ministry Conflict: A Parable on How Resistance Can Be Your Ally* (Grand Rapids, MI: Zondervan, 2005).

19

AN OPEN INVITATION FOR REMISSIONING LEADERS

I disdained to be a little beginner. Puffed up with
pride, I considered myself a mature adult.

AUGUSTINE, *CONFESSIONS*

The special courage it takes to experience true belonging is not just
about braving the wilderness, it's about becoming *the wilderness. It's*
about breaking down the walls, abandoning our ideological bunkers,
and living from our wild heart rather than our weary hurt.

BRENÉ BROWN, *BRAVING THE WILDERNESS*

REMISSIONING A CHURCH ISN'T FLASHY, easy, fun, or hip. In fact, the more flashy, easy, fun, or hip you try to make things, the more pushback you will often experience.

At the core of remissioning churches is a deep missional impulse that requires multiple conversions. The first conversion is for the church leadership to shift from wanting to make converts/consumers or get more Christians from other churches into the pews and classes. This is a conversion to a new *telos*: a new vision of what faithfulness and fruitfulness look like for your church. The second conversion is to a missional life for the sake of the world and your neighbors—and yourself. The second conversion is a shift from making church about eternal rescue plans to living out the prayer of God's kingdom being on earth as in heaven. This doesn't mean we are not concerned about matters of eternity, but it is a shift from trying to escape this world to working for the renewal of the world (see Rev 21:1-5; 22:1-5). Remissioned churches have discovered a new mission to help people learn to become disciples of Jesus as they, too, follow Jesus.

I'm writing as a Protestant senior pastor of a 165-plus-year-old Baptist church, which feels overwhelming enough—so I can only imagine how challenging it must be to consider change within the two-thousand-year-old Roman Catholic church. Susan Bigelow Reynolds writes about her experiences in helping remission a parish church in Boston:

> There is a saying, popular in intentional communities, that goes, "Everybody wants a revolution, but nobody wants to do the dishes." The year I spent keeping the lights on in that Roxbury parish house taught me to do the dishes, literally and metaphorically. In certain ways, St. Mary of the Angels . . . was, among many other things, a sort of refuge for Boston Catholics who found themselves hanging on to their faith by a thread in the wake of the 2002 abuse crisis. And yet what I learned from the community's longtime leaders is that changing the culture of power in a 2,000-year-old institution means resisting the urge to burn the whole rotten thing to the ground and instead sticking around and going to meetings and participating in the often infuriatingly slow work of change.[1]

Reynolds describes the drip, drip, drip of leading established churches into new ways of being on mission with God. It isn't flashy. It is a slow, steady work in a particular direction that seeks to make disciples who embody the life, death, and resurrection of Jesus and the sentness of the Spirit. Remissioning leadership recognizes that while your church may pine for change, proclaim it wants young families, and declare its openness to new ways of being church, leaders must recognize that many people don't want to do the work: dishes, laundry, grass cutting—sitting in a new pew, mixing generations and learning styles, navigating conflict, showing up with their neighbors.

Remembering that "everybody wants a revolution, but nobody wants to do the dishes" can help you recalibrate your expectations as a leader. Remissioning asks you to resist the temptation to create celebrity pastors and leaders. It challenges the notion that leaders are the experts who have all the answers and carry the vision on behalf of the entire group. Most of all, it requires you to understand the difference between who you are as a person and your role in the organization.

As a senior pastor of an established church, I am tempted to believe the adoring things people say about me and my work and ignore the criticisms. Or, vice versa, I am tempted to think I am all the critical things people say and ignore the positive. In reality, "pastors have to realize that they are the repositories of the hopes, dreams, and aspirations of their followers. . . . The danger comes when you start to believe that what they are seeing in you is actually you."[2] Remissioning leaders differentiate between the role and the self while being mindful of the temptation to conflate role and authority and short-circuit the work of real leadership—that is, change from the inside out.

There is a story that Roman emperor Marcus Aurelius hired an assistant to follow him as he walked throughout the empire and whisper in his ears, after he'd been praised by the people, "You are just a man. You are just a man." As tempting as it is to believe the hype, churches need people to emphasize the importance of washing the dishes together. No matter your budget, your role, your attendance, your salary—you are just a woman; you are just a man. Don't confuse your role in the organization with your spiritual or emotional health.

ESSENTIAL QUALITIES OF REMISSIONING LEADERS

Remissioning leaders empower people to experience their own transformation for the sake of their community and the flourishing of their neighborhoods and world. These types of leaders aren't about amassing power, becoming the visionary, developing a celebrity following, or simply growing church numbers. Remissioning leaders are about creating opportunity for spiritual, emotional, physical, and communal transformation so the mission of God might flourish.

Here are a few characteristics that are helpful for remissioning leaders to develop and practice in their own lives and to cultivate in various leadership communities in the church.

Vulnerability. Brené Brown gets at the heart of vulnerability with this question: "Are we willing to show up and be seen when we can't control the outcome?"[3] Vulnerability as a leader is scary, especially in established churches where the people may not be used to a pastor transgressing the barrier between leader and follower. But without vulnerability, it becomes impossible for a church to experience transformation. Vulnerability in leadership and within the church are crucial to remissioning. Vulnerability helps you shift into a with-ness that flattens hierarchical power structures and creates a posture of repentance, learning, and perpetual transformation.

Remissioning is a vulnerable process that depends on vulnerable leaders. It means admitting that your church has things to learn about itself and ways it must embrace the cross so new life will be possible. It is an inherently vulnerable and exposing journey to choose to lay down power and learn from others.

Polycentric power. Polycentric leadership moves from the head of the table to a round table. Instead of being the ones who make every decision, polycentric leaders emphasize making disciples, and the disciples are the church. When multiple centers of authority are connected to each other through shared mission, mutual submission, and the Spirit, power is diffused throughout the whole church instead of centralized in one group, committee, staff, or leader. Eun Strawser's upcoming book on sharing power and distributed leadership explores how authority in decision-making, relational influence, and accomplishment can be matured through collaboration.

In this way, leadership is about much more than making decisions. We focus on formation, discipleship, and cultivating kingdom imagination. And instead of a church falling apart when a lead pastor resigns, polycentric leadership situates the leadership back into the core of the church and the relational trust that grows through apprenticeship and shared decision-making. Giving away power, taking on the form of a servant, and making space for others to lead creates a vacuum for others to grow and fill.

Willingness to risk. Tod Bolsinger's book *Canoeing The Mountains* is inspired by the journey of Lewis and Clark to discover a water passageway from the East Coast to the West Coast for trade. The problem was none of their maps worked, and the passageway didn't exist. But instead of turning around and heading home, Lewis and Clark explored on and charted new territory they would never have seen if they had stopped going. Remissioning leadership requires you to risk and explore new ways for your church to be faithful to the mission of God in your context—even when your maps are wrong and the next right step isn't clear.

You will lose some people during the remissioning journey. When you prioritize kingdom over partisan politics, some people will leave. When you prioritize loving your neighbors over creating holy huddles, some people will leave. When you ask people to lay down their preferences for a bigger mission, some people will leave.

Change requires risk and the risk means that not everyone will stay. But the risk of staying the same is you will continue down the path you are already on, and that is itself a risk. Which risk will help you chase after the *telos* God has put on your heart and the heart of your church?

Receiving the work as a gift. Contrary to the CEO pastor model, remissioning leaders practice humility and hold their work with an open hand, receiving as a gift from the Spirit this journey with a group of people for the sake of a larger mission. This isn't to say there aren't hard days, and I mean incredibly hard, but your posture as a leader will help set the tone for the journey. If you can remember you are the thermostat for the temperature, it helps you differentiate between the good and bad things people say about you and remember that your identity is rooted in your adoption as a daughter or son of God. While remissioning a church is one of the hardest things anyone can do, it is still a gift. It has the potential to transform you and your church as it awakens to the mission of God for the sake of its community. Keeping that vision in front of you can help you pause and remember the gift that the Creator of the universe invites you into this work as a way of sharing in the mission.

Self-awareness. There is a world of difference between self-consciousness and self-awareness. Self-conscious leaders have a hard time separating what people say about them and the image they project from who they are. Self-awareness is the process of learning to go beneath the surface of one's life to discover the motivations, patterns, joys, sins, pains, hopes, dreams, and desires that shape your actions and leadership. Leaders who intentionally take steps to grow in their self-awareness embody the expectation for the church that we are never "finished" but that we continue to grow, learn, and develop throughout our whole lives.

Remissioning leaders recognize that the transformation of their churches depends on the Spirit and our willingness to submit our lives to the possibility of transformation before expecting others to change first. The days of Christendom are behind us, and our maps no longer work. Are you willing to develop new maps and explore uncharted territory both in yourself and with your church for the sake of your community?

GROWING MATURE REMISSIONING LEADERSHIP

A mission-critical maturity marker of remissioning leadership is a clear plan for apprenticeship and leadership succession. There was a time in church history when the senior pastor was the resident expert on most things: preaching, pastoral care, theology, worship, missions. This lead voice was the prominent voice in the community. But as culture has evolved and the diversity of leadership found in the Scriptures has been more deeply explored, church leadership conversations have changed as well.

Perhaps centralized, hierarchical, programmatic, individually based leadership worked well for generations of church in the West, but we might ask whether it has created disciples who reflect the *telos* anyone had in mind. If organizations are perfectly designed to get the results they are getting, the same is true about our leadership models. The hierarchical leadership form and its negation, flat leadership, have created the churches we find ourselves in today.

Hierarchical leadership is the typical approach to leadership in the church in the United States. The senior pastor is the visionary leader who brings down the vision from on high, and their primary task is to get folks on board to accomplish the vision. The senior leader carries the main vision, knowledge, and truth for where the church is headed. The measurements for success are financial resources, building size, and numbers of people.

The flip side of hierarchical leadership is flat leadership. In this model, which came about because of negative experiences with hierarchical leadership, the different weights and authorities between various leadership voices are eliminated. Flat leadership tends to be anti-institutional with great sensitivity to power and the dangers of elevated voices in a community.

Flat leadership creates a vacuum in hopes that people will step into the void. This kind of leadership can feel fuzzy and difficult to describe because it is characterized by an unfocused mission. Flat leadership usually results in stagnant mission as no one person or group of people is given space to lead.

There is another option besides the top-down approach or flat leadership. In remissioning churches leadership is polycentric, shared across various centers within the church and even at times from the outside in. Polycentric leadership emphasizes communal formation and is focused on how leadership is multiplied and reproduced in disciples.

Polycentric leadership creates space for APEST to come into focus, as particular voices form a choral symphony of leadership. If each person is gifted into the fivefold typology—apostle, prophet, evangelist, shepherd, teacher—then part of your responsibility in helping your church remission is to elevate and accentuate voices of leadership that are typically quieted or marginalized in your context. This work of mutual submission to make room for different capacities of leadership begins with the person with the most power in your church. If the senior leadership is unwilling or incapable of making room at the table for different voices of leadership to emerge, it will be a challenge to remission.

Remissioning churches learn to reflect this polycentric power in their leadership structure. In my Baptist context, it used to be that all pastoral care, administrative responsibilities, and strategic thinking went through the same leadership group: deacons. The group meant to provide spiritual and practical support for church members in times of change, celebration, and difficulty was somehow also playing the roles of apostles, evangelists, and prophets. When we clarified how the deacons could model healthy shepherding and reduce the need for them to also make decisions about HVAC units and financial policies along with leading through change, our church members were served exponentially better than when the deacons were stretched too thin by too many responsibilities.

Polycentric leadership takes practice and intentionality, as well as character and regular habits of formation. Core to this kind of leadership is the willingness to practice mutual submission. This kind of leadership is often countercultural, as Jesus points out to his followers: "You know that those who are regarded as rulers of the Gentiles lord it over them, and their high officials exercise authority over them. Not so with you. Instead, whoever wants to become great among you must be your servant, and whoever wants to be first must be slave of all. For even the Son of Man did not come to be served, but to serve, and to give his life as a ransom for many" (Mk 10:42-45).

Creating polycentric leadership will require the senior pastor and leaders to intentionally give away power and put more responsibility in the hands of the people so that they can participate more as citizens than consumers. It means that instead of a church being dominated by the leadership of the senior pastor, it reflects a holistic system that has room for all APEST functions.

One challenge to pay attention to is the tendency for established churches to struggle with the senior pastor sharing leadership instead of operating in a hierarchical manner. This can easily happen across generational lines or with folks who have church experiences in settings where there is an emphasis on hierarchy. Remember that this kind of recalibration of culture takes time, intentional conversations, and drip, drip, drip leadership.

FURTHER READING

Brené Brown, *Braving the Wilderness: The Quest for True Belonging and the Courage to Stand Alone* (New York: Random House, 2017).

20

A REMISSIONING PATH REQUIRES NEW METRICS

The outcomes we need are those deep, and even disturbingly clear,
descriptions of what we believe can be different if God gets involved.
Again, this is no longer problem solving, it is possibility hunting.

GIL RENDLE, *DOING THE MATH OF MISSION*

A great organization is one that delivers superior performance and
makes a distinctive impact over a long period of time. For a business,
financial returns are a perfectly legitimate measure of performance.
For a social sector organization, however, performance must be
assessed relative to mission, not financial returns. In the social sectors,
the critical question is not "How much money do we make per dollar
of invested capital?" but "How effectively do we deliver on our mission
and make a distinctive impact, relative to our resources?"

JIM COLLINS, *GOOD TO GREAT*

Non-profit organizations have no "bottom line." They are prone to
consider everything they do to be righteous and moral and to serve a cause,
so they are not willing to say, if it doesn't produce results then maybe we
should direct our resources elsewhere. Non-profit organizations need the
discipline of organized abandonment perhaps even more than a business
does. They need to face up to critical choices . . . the starting point is to
recognize that change is not a threat. It's an opportunity.

PETER DRUCKER, *MANAGING THE NONPROFIT ORGANIZATION*

QUESTIONS ABOUT WHAT TO MEASURE, how to measure, and why to measure aren't easy for nonprofits or churches. The longer a church is around, the easier it is to get fuzzy on your mission, what to count, and how to tell if your hoped-for outcomes are being accomplished. And since asking questions about how to honor tradition and culture is connected to our identity and community, it's not easy to know how to measure movement in our churches or neighborhoods. Much of the discussion around metrics in church life has to do with easily measured things like money and attendance, but often those things are separate from the hoped-for outcome or *telos* of your church's discipleship pathways.

The questions we ask and attempt to answer as leaders and churches give shape to who we are and who we are becoming. If our most meaningful questions are: "How many people attend our worship service?" "How much money are we bringing in?" and "How many programs do we have each week?" we can get good at counting but poor at measuring transformation.

Earlier in the change cycle we asked: *Do we have a mission worth dying for?* After breakthrough we asked: *Do we have a mission worth living for?* These questions are meaningfully connected to how we gauge remissioning. They reveal the end goal of our personal leadership, the spiritual and emotional health of our community, the impetus to put mission above preferences, and how our churches make disciples. Ultimately, these questions shift our work from creating spectators, consumers, and attenders to producing citizens, disciples, and leaders. These orienting questions are different from those about things that are easily quantified. They reveal our true goals, and they act as signposts of fruitfulness and faithfulness in our personal, communal, missional, and discipleship contexts.

Gil Rendle's *Doing the Math of Mission* is a helpful, prophetic, and important read for churches that want to seriously consider new metrics for church life. Rendle makes an important distinction between counting and measuring. Counting is paying attention to numbers, answering questions like "How many?" in terms of resources such as people, money, or space. Measuring is giving attention to change, asking questions like "How far?" in terms of our progress toward our goals.[1] Rendle writes:

> Countables are easily quantifiable. We know how many resources we have and how many activities we pursue. We can number and report these even as we argue their importance.

Measurables are more dependent on descriptions of what we feel called to and hope to be able to produce. If we can describe the change that we are called to make, then we can also have discerning conversation about whether we are moving toward that change over time.[2]

Counting and measuring are both important in healthy remissioning metrics. Major problems arise when we make the countables the measuring tool or when we fail to measure at all. Churches that quantify and spend time counting but fail to measure the outcomes of their activities and attendance lack clarity around their purpose. Churches that measure transformation without an accurate counting of people and other resources have difficulty knowing if their work is reproducible.

To follow a remissioning path, we need to develop new metrics that help us distinguish between what we can count and what we can measure, while differentiating between inputs, outputs, and outcomes. This is the aim of the model shown in figure 20.1.

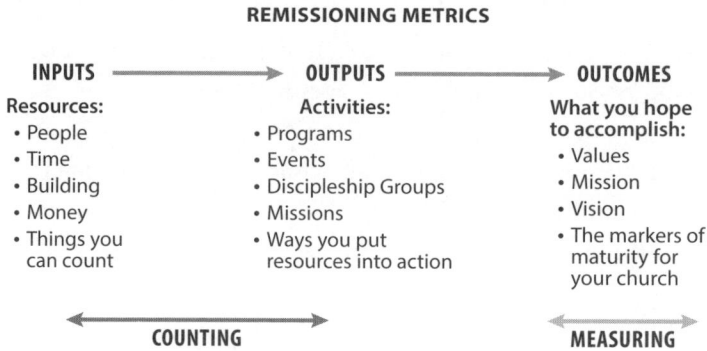

REMISSIONING METRICS

INPUTS ⟶	OUTPUTS ⟶	OUTCOMES
Resources:	Activities:	What you hope to accomplish:
• People	• Programs	• Values
• Time	• Events	• Mission
• Building	• Discipleship Groups	• Vision
• Money	• Missions	• The markers of maturity for your church
• Things you can count	• Ways you put resources into action	

⟵ COUNTING ⟶   ⟵ MEASURING ⟶

Figure 20.1. Remissioning metrics

Inputs. Inputs are the resources you need to pursue outcomes (markers of maturity) in your church. These are things you can count, such as people, time, building space, and money. You can't remission without inputs. Paying attention to shifts in money, building usage, time, attendance numbers, and other tangibles is important. For example, when we host a trunk-or-treat for our suburban-rural community on campus, we know that up to a thousand people will come through to get candy, visit a food truck, and have a nice evening together. Therefore we will need a certain number of "trunks," bathrooms, food trucks, parking spaces, bags of candy, trashcans, and microphones. These inputs are critical to being good neighbors and hosting events.

The problem is when churches confuse their inputs (money, people, or number of activities) as a sign of health or maturity. We all know churches with plenty of money and people that don't look or act like Jesus. Counting inputs and outputs and thinking that is the end of the story is to misunderstand the aim of remissioning. But paying attention to your inputs helps you have clarity in the planning of your outputs.

Outputs. Outputs are the activities that put your inputs into practice. Outputs create shared habits that grow our maturity in the remissioning process. For example, your discipleship groups are determined by the number of mature leaders you have to lead. Your events are based on the resources you have within your church to serve others. The outputs are the "how" of the remissioning process. They shape the pathway toward our outcomes.

You can count the number of times you lead a program, how many discipleship groups you have going on, and the different ways people are invited to live in mission. And it's important to match the inputs to the outputs so we are living wisely and intentionally toward our hoped-for outcomes.

Outcomes. Outcomes are the describable, clearly defined markers of maturity your church believes God has called you to for the next season of your shared life. The outcomes are the ways your church measures progress on its *telos*. Without a commitment to put the inputs and outputs toward a particular end goal, it's impossible to know if your event, discipleship group, or mission pathway is accomplishing the goal. For example, if your church wants to decrease the number of people experiencing food insecurity in your community and year over year the number of people you serve in your food pantry increases rather than decreases, how do you know if you are making a dent in food security issues in your community?

When you name and describe an outcome, it's helpful to give it a time frame (how long you discern it will take you to see it accomplished), describe what your maturity markers look like in the lives of disciples (often your church's values), and what inputs and outputs are necessary to accomplish the outcome. The world is changing quickly, and outcomes aren't meant to stay the same forever. Having clear time frames will be helpful in later pruning processes too!

It's helpful to have these metrics in mind as you think about where your church is in its life cycle. They also help you build mission funding plans (budgets), clearer and more intentional activities, and more sustainable outcomes.

The process of creating new metrics to distinguish between counting and measuring is the difference between making converts and disciples. God's hopes and dreams for your remissioned church are much greater than large numbers of people consuming religious goods and services. People are being invited into a whole new way of life with Jesus as Lord. So a few helpful questions for you to consider as you create new metrics are:

- What ways of counting and measuring in your context will need to be carried forward in your remissioning?
- What ways of counting and measuring will need to be disrupted?
- How will you create a discipleship process to develop new metrics in light of the disruption?
- What outcomes is your church seeking after together?
- Where have you confused counting and measuring?

The default in most churches is to focus on things we can count. In remissioning we need to develop a more holistic picture of what the renewal of all things looks like—and how our churches can lead people there. Instead of asking "What is our weekly attendance?" or "How much is our annual giving?" here are some alternative metric questions that can help measure clear outcomes. Try asking:

- What percentage of our budget helps our church practice each of our values? (Try creating a chart that demonstrates where your dollars go in terms of practicing and maturing the values in your church.)
- Where have our people taken steps to enter new spaces of belonging?
- What stories of thanks have been shared from our community about the way our church practices its faith in public?
- What markers of maturity have we seen grow in our church this year?
- What organizational gaps have been closed so that fewer people fall through the cracks?

- Where have we seen our leadership take a communal step of maturity this year?
- Where have we seen meaningful repentance in our church this year?
- What values have moved from aspirational to practiced in our church?
- How do the things we can count inform the way we measure?
- How has our church practiced a communal rule of life?

These questions help us focus our priorities, understand movement in people's lives, and know the difference between things we count and things we measure.

21

FOUR PATHWAYS FOR REMISSIONING

We must come to see that human progress never rolls in on wheels of inevitability. It comes through the tireless efforts and persistent work of men willing to be coworkers with God, and without this hard work time itself becomes an ally of the forces of social stagnation. We must use time creatively, and forever realize that the time is always ripe to do right.

MARTIN LUTHER KING JR.,
"LETTER FROM BIRMINGHAM JAIL"

TO CHART A PATH OF TRANSFORMATION requires continued awareness of where your church is in the church life cycle and to choose the necessary route back to health.[1] This process relies on creative destruction, i.e., embracing the cross as a pathway to new life, but has different costs associated with each path. The remissioning project isn't simply to return to the health and vitality side of the life cycle—it is to grow the discipling practices that help churches learn how to disrupt themselves before the process of decline, dropout, and death. Can church leaders learn to embrace the cross and experience resurrection breakthrough earlier in the life cycle so we might have less generational turnover and a sustainable mission? Let's look at the possible pathways of creative destruction in figure 21.1 that make up the remissioning journey.

REMISSIONING PATHWAYS

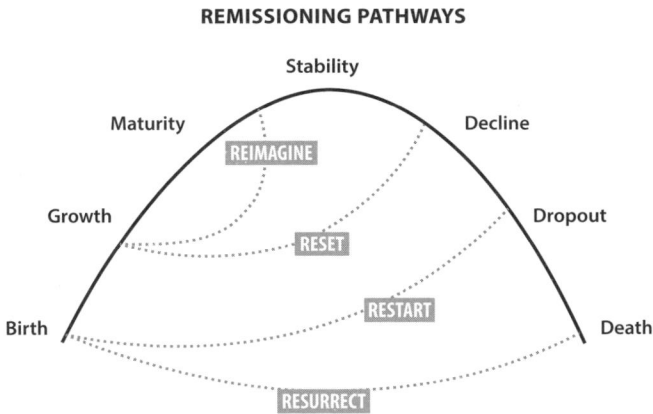

Figure 21.1. Remissioning pathways

REIMAGINE

A church that is on the path of reimagination intentionally disrupts its own successful inputs and outputs as the outcomes shift with time and new inputs and outputs need to be developed and deployed. This is a challenging mindset to adopt, because it feels counterintuitive to disrupt growth and stability to remain in a posture of regular learning and reformation, but churches that make reimagination a habit will develop people who see creative destruction as part of discipleship. The outcome of this process is disciples who embrace the cross as a pathway to new life instead of believing that endless amassing of resources without pruning will work in the long term.

Flatlands Reformed Church in Brooklyn, New York, was founded in 1654 by a group of white settlers who wanted to start a Reformed church connected to the Netherlands in the colonies. FRC has gone through several rounds on the life cycle over the years, and for most of its history it has been a white congregation. When the church first called Pastor Paul Glover, they anticipated a resurrection project. They believed that Pastor Paul would serve as a chaplain to the established church while planting a new congregation representing the diversity of the neighborhood, and this new church would eventually occupy the original campus. However, Pastor Paul brought all the energy, creative thinking, and love for the community intended for church planting into the established church, and Flatlands came back to life.[2]

As FRC regained its strength, grew more committed to making disciples, and saw breakthrough in its local community, reimagination took hold of both pastor and congregation. Instead of going through a resurrection process via a church plant, they allowed holy disruption to inspire fresh experiences in worship, purposeful resourcing in the community, and renewed emphasis on living "in" with one another to grow more mature disciples in FRC. The church flourished in its diversity and multicultural expressions of worship and disciple-making. It was counterintuitive to use the new movement to reimagine the existing congregation, but it was that willingness to change course that brought Flatlands back into a season of growth spiritually and numerically.

Some of the markers of this reimagination included clarifying their community partners: working with local nonprofits to alleviate food insecurity, creating a comprehensive English-as-second-language program for immigrants in their neighborhood, and partnering to care for children facing crisis. While it would have been easier for FRC to stay the course and pursue a pathway of resurrection, they chose a pathway of reimagination that led to momentum on the growth side of the life cycle.

RESET

In this pathway, churches have to recalibrate because they have gotten distracted from their mission and are experiencing decline. The decline could be in inputs or outputs or the outcomes needing to change and the church being too slow to adapt. This pathway involves conversations around counting that help reveal the need for a shift in outcome.

Resetting an institution is the least destructive experience on the descent, but the effect is the same for an institution whether it's restarting, resetting, or resurrecting: the outcome has moved to a new location, and a new pathway is required to find it. Institutions that need to reset have a decreased clarity of mission and means to achieve that mission. An institution that needs a reset is one that has experienced some degree of "mission drift," as Greg Jones describes it:

> Mission drift occurs when the work separates from the identity. The phenomenon is something quite different from, and less obviously perceptible than, not having a mission, losing a mission or giving up on a mission.[3]

To reset, an institution must return to the beginning of its story and examine what it is measuring as success, then put those measurements against the backdrop of its imagined future. Often institutions that need to reset have begun to measure the wrong habits or outcomes.

St. Luke's in East London's Canning Town is situated in a parish that is so diverse there is no majority culture. Over the years the church has changed along with the neighborhood. Most of the housing was originally built when workers flooded to the area to work at the Royal Docks, and St. Luke's was created in response to an article in a journal edited by Charles Dickens that highlighted the terrible housing and work conditions. Only three miles from the center of London, much of the community is public housing and a third of it has been torn down and rebuilt. With no majority culture and dramatic changes in the community over the years, it can be difficult for the church to know how to hold things together.[4]

As a way to get out of its decaying building, St. Luke's sold its largest asset and partnered with the local authorities to rebuild a school in the community. Under the leadership of Reverend Amy Stott, the church has recognized that amidst so much diversity and change, they could build bridges with nonprofits, other churches, government, and local businesses for the good of the whole community. On a trip to the UK, I brought other pastors to learn from St. Luke's and marveled at the way the neighbors celebrated Reverend Stott's leadership, celebrated the impact of the school, and described St. Luke's as a church where they could find family when so many had moved away from home. Over the course of a few years St. Luke's has transitioned from numerical decline and lack of mission clarity to become a church for young families, adults looking for a home away from home, and anyone seeking connection and joy. As a result of its reset, St. Luke's can name the way it is on mission and neighbors seek its leadership during difficult losses in the community. Bridge-making churches help previously disconnected groups find one another, and this church has become indispensable to its neighbors.

To reset an institution, leaders must be in place who can read the institutional outcomes and habits before an overhaul of culture becomes necessary. If institutions can ask questions essential to traditioned innovation, creative destruction can become a means of reset:

For it returns us to basic questions that all organizations, for-profit or not, must ask: Why must we exist? What do we do that no one else can do as well? What would be lost if we disappeared?[5]

Reset is a way to clarify the mission, create measurements of success, and calibrate habits toward the strategic end. Institutions that need to reset have experienced seasons of growth, health, and vitality but have moved past a point of stability into a state of decline. Institutions that embrace a reset will avoid a thoroughgoing destruction as they form new habits to measure success for their strategic end.

Restart

This pathway is more extensive, requiring a new *telos* or mission for your church that will result in significant recalibration of resources and activities. If we hold to be true the maxim, "Your organization is perfectly designed to achieve the results it is currently getting," then a new mission/purpose/*telos* will result in major shifts throughout the rest of the church. During this phase people drop out, resources and activities wane, and the mission becomes impossible to see.

One church that restarted in Alexandria, Virginia, is now called Convergence. But it began in 1946 as Fair-Park Baptist Church. In its heyday, Fair-Park experienced growth, innovation, and creativity, which are clearly seen in the church's colorful sanctuary, skillful use of light, and creative use of space and buildings. But after fifty years there was a significant decline in inputs and outputs, which resulted in Fair-Park merging with Duke Street Baptist. Yet the congregation still experienced decline. In 2005, the church recognized that it was no longer connecting with its community and sought new leadership.[6]

In 2006 Fair-Park invited Lisa Cole Smith, a recent graduate of the John Leland Center for Theological Studies—also an actor, director, and artist—to consider submitting a proposal to restart Fair-Park as an experimental church. With a unique vision for combining the practices of church and art, Convergence was born out of an intentional process of creative destruction. As it asked a central question, "What would happen at the intersection of art, faith, and human experience?" the church acquired the building and property, along with initial funding to innovate, and restarted under a different name. Over the last ten years Convergence has blossomed into a creative community of faith where art and spirituality live in relationship with one another, and it has become a safe place for exploration for the community at large.[7]

Relying on the creative and generous tradition of Fair-Park, Convergence brought new life to a congregation that had previously lacked hope. Convergence restarted the heart of Fair-Park while helping it faithfully innovate into a future it would not have seen had it not been willing to die to a version of itself. In that death, a door was opened and the wind changed direction:

> By opening our doors to local artists and arts organizations and creating a forum for public dialogue on faith and cultural issues we believe we will be better equipped to meet current and future challenges. We want to encourage more churches to do this so we no longer feel the need to "catch up" or battle culture and so that artists have a truly valued place in society; neither celebrity nor misfit, but humble contributor with a credible voice. We hope this creative convergence will promote a society whose culture reflects the deep spiritual and existential concerns of all people and promotes the human experience as one dedicated to higher purposes.[8]

Restarts never happen on blank slates, but they involve a process of creative destruction that relies on loosening the tether to the past in order to imagine a new future. Convergence helps institutions realize that without regular practice of traditioned innovation over the years, they can lose touch with their surrounding community and fail to make the connections necessary to create clusters of shared value. Fair-Park's willingness to lay down its building, time, history, and understanding of itself for a larger mission and purpose is a generative practice of creative destruction that fosters hope.

RESURRECT

This is the most thorough kind of remissioning process. It requires that an institution die to one way of existence in order to experience rebirth. The scope of change and transformation is deep and wide in an institution that experiences death in order to embark on a journey of new life. First, leadership must change throughout the institution. The further along the decline and death trajectory the institution is, the greater the change that must happen throughout every tier of the organization. Not only must top executives or lead pastors step down or be let go, but managers and change agents likely need to exit as well. Because the breadth of change begins at the center and moves to the margins, a leadership overhaul is essential for a resurrected future.

A new culture is possible only when there is a deliberate death of one institution for the sake of creating a new *telos* and means to achieve it. Resurrecting an institution requires an active imagination, first to cultivate a memory that holds the stories of past success loosely, recognizing that these stories may need to be reinterpreted in the context of death. Then, good translators who can recontextualize the institution for the sake of a new *telos* will be essential for institutional rebirth. This process will likely include a change in name, identity, governing stories, and tethered relationships, all part of the branding or storying process, along with the overhaul of leadership.

Institutional resurrection is the most challenging, wide-sweeping, and tumultuous expression of creative destruction. It is painful, all-encompassing, and relentless. But when the process of creative destruction can be embraced, the smell of death can be overwhelmed by the fragrance of new life.

An example of resurrection is St. John's Catholic Church, which was founded in 1856 and constructed its building in 1858 in Louisville, Kentucky. At the time, the Roman Catholic population was surging throughout the city, and for the first service over twenty-five hundred people arrived for the consecration of the building and mass. After more than one hundred years, the church experienced changes after Vatican II and the population began to trickle away. Eventually, the church found the courage to ask the city of Louisville if there were any pressing problems their building might help to solve. In 1984, St. John's and the city formed a task force to address the number of homeless individuals living in the city. In 1986, St John's sold its building to the city of Louisville for one dollar. In the death of the church, a homeless day shelter for men was birthed. The city had seen men who had places to stay at night die on the streets during the day because they had nowhere warm to stay during daylight hours.[9]

St. John's conversion from a church to the St. John Center for Homeless Men has become a signpost in the city for what creative destruction can look like when it happens in the context of collaborative relationships. The death of a particular church gave birth to a group of people being church while resourcing the community to meet a real need. The death of one institution and its resurrection into another has literally brought new life to the city. Homeless men who faced the threat of dying can now stay somewhere warm, safe, and hopeful during the day. The center partners with other agencies and together they are making gains on eliminating homelessness throughout the city.[10]

Gaining clarity on its path can help your church assess the means necessary to cultivate new life. Ultimately, the church is not our church but is God's church. Clarifying how resources, activities, and outcomes connect (see table 21.1) doesn't guarantee success! But lack of intentional reflection on this process can lead to the reproduction of malformed disciples.

Table 21.1. How resources, activities, and outcomes connect in remissioning pathways

Pathway	Inputs	Outputs	Outcome
Reimagine	Resources that are helping achieve previous outcomes are working	Activities that help achieve previous outcomes are working	New outcomes are emerging that will cause a shift of inputs and outputs
Reset	Decline in the resources available	Decline in participation and connection to activities that help achieve outcomes	New outcomes are necessary as the previous outcomes were achieved or shifted
Restart	Major decline in the resources available	Major decline in activities with a clear sense of mission	Major overhaul of outcomes from a clear mission is necessary
Resurrect	Clear shift to new resources	Clear shift to new activities	New mission/purpose and new outcomes

MAKE A PLAN

With a team of people, take some time to evaluate which pathway of remissioning you believe your congregation will need to consider. Do you need to reimagine, reset, restart, or resurrect? Why?

If you were to create a plan with other leaders that took into account where your church is in the remissioning process and your own leadership journey, what would you describe?

- What needs to stop?
- What needs to start?
- What are the next steps?

If you were to make a short-term plan (six to twelve months) and then a long-term plan (one to three years), what would it look like? Some areas to consider exploring as you answer those questions:

- Personal—your own leadership; emotional, physical, and spiritual health
- Church culture—committees, worship, sense of mission, etc. that you want to exegete
- Community culture—businesses, partnerships, resources, relationships to exegete
- Conflict to be navigated
- Skunkworks/divine experiments to try
- Discipleship pathways
- Leadership dynamics (strengths and shadows)
- Themes to explore together as a church

Lastly, name the outcomes you hope will develop in this plan. Be as specific as you can. What does "fruitfulness" or "success" or "hitting the mark" look like? How will you measure your work?

For both long-term and short-term descriptions, be clear and succinct. Be specific and realistic about the length of time it will take to do the work. It's helpful to recalibrate volunteer and staff position descriptions so you can purposefully name the ways you are evolving the role, authority, and duties of the pastoral staff. Keep in mind that you will have to disappoint people at a rate they can absorb, but without adjusting the metrics for our leaders, we often create an impossible environment where they try to keep everything they were doing and take on new responsibilities at the same time.

Some simple advice: don't waste interruptions. If you have changeover in staff or opportunity to revise job descriptions, bylaws, or policy manuals, don't waste the chance to reframe the metrics you are using as a church to evaluate health, vitality, and maturity. When churches recalibrate expectations for what it looks like to be church and live on mission with diverse leadership skills, the metrics for remissioning are shared by the whole instead of living in the mind of a select few.

Remissioning Summary

A helpful exercise as you go on this journey is to keep a running one- to two-page document that helps you keep in mind what you are pursuing in the remissioning process. Using the questions below, can you clearly describe where your church is on the remissioning journey? Can you describe this to your church as well, so they know how to take the next steps with you?

- What pathway does your church need to consider in order to experience new life: reimagine, reset, restart, or resurrect?
- Give a brief explanation why it needs to choose that path.
- What spiritual practices will help you remain grounded as a leader while putting this into practice?

Think of this as your one-page summary or elevator pitch to let folks know why remissioning should take place in your context.

Further Reading

Gil Rendle, *Doing the Math of Mission: Fruits, Faithfulness, and Metrics* (Lanham, MD: Rowman & Littlefield, 2014).

Jim Collins, *Good to Great and the Social Sectors: A Monograph to Accompany Good to Great* (New York: HarperBusiness, 2005).

Les McKeown, *Predictable Success: Getting Your Organization on the Growth Track—and Keeping It There* (Austin, TX: Greenleaf Book Group, 2014).

Peter Drucker, *Managing the Nonprofit Organization: Principles and Practices* (New York: HarperBusiness, 2006).

22

DYING TO LIVE

To foster communities that are aimed toward the right end—to lead communities that thrive as foretastes of the kingdom of God—we need a deep, abiding direction. And Scripture, which actively orders and reorders our thoughts, teaching us how to think and live, exerts the kind of pressure that gives us this direction.

GREG JONES AND KAVIN ROWE, *THRIVING COMMUNITIES*

The ability to face constructively the tension of opposing ideas and, instead of choosing one at the expense of the other, generate a creative resolution of the tension in the form of a new idea that contains elements of the opposing ideas but is superior to each.

ROGER MARTIN, *THE OPPOSABLE MIND*

REMISSIONING ESTABLISHED CHURCHES from the inside out is not the easy road. It relies on leaders who cultivate a spirituality of weakness while stewarding their churches instead of trying to own them. Remissioning involves creative destruction—the intentional disruption, pruning, and death of programs, resources, and activities—to make room for new life. While developing a clearer sense of mission, churches also practice traditioned innovation—remembering the best of where they have come from and using the healthiest parts of that past for a new future. At the heart of practicing creative destruction and traditioned innovation is the hope of better discipleship pathways that will develop citizens of the kingdom instead of consumers of religious goods and services. To do this, remissioning leaders depend on practicing adaptive leadership, which meets people where they are and invites them into a new future through intentional habits, conflict, and shared power.

Perhaps the hardest part of this road is the shift to new healthy metrics. Established churches love to count—people, money, attendance, programs, activities—but often struggle to measure whether any real transformation is taking place or if their work is making a sustainable impact on the community. The hard road is learning to keep the end in mind and then make the necessary shifts in activities and resourcing to make meaningful progress toward that end.

The invitation to remission an established church is birthed out of the way Jesus lived out the mission with us. Eugene Peterson of *The Message* interprets the opening of John's Gospel like this:

> The Word became flesh and blood,
>   and moved into the neighborhood.
> We saw the glory with our own eyes,
>   the one-of-a-kind glory,
>   like Father, like Son,
> Generous inside and out,
>   true from start to finish. (John 1:14 MSG)

One of the healthiest remissioning churches I know is Christ City Church in Washington, DC. Their vision is "to see the flourishing of God's kingdom on display in every life and every sphere of life, in DC and beyond." They have worked hard to be clear in their practices and values so they might live more fully on mission with God in their community. Christ City is a church plant that has been around long enough to remission. They reimagine themselves regularly through disruption so they don't mistake stability for faithfulness. The diversity of their staff and leadership reflects the community where they live and serve. Their volunteer page clarifies the why and how of their mission: "Place matters. Because Jesus took on flesh and blood, lived in a neighborhood and identified with a people, we also root ourselves in neighborhoods and identify with people. Our place is Washington, DC. While many come to this city to consume it and to use it, we want to be among those who love it."[1]

Over the past five years Christ City has reorganized its staff, added and clarified partnerships, pursued tangible expressions of justice, and regularly innovated in the ways it makes disciples. One of the hallmarks of the remissioning journey has been the intentional pursuit of polycentric leadership and distribution of authority among the staff team. While many churches wait until things get difficult or experience significant decline, Christ City models the central heartbeat of remissioning: disciple death and resurrection into our churches earlier in the life cycle for the sake of mission in our neighborhoods.

I just crossed the line of twenty years serving on church staffs. For eleven years I served a church plant and for nearly ten years I've participated in remissioning an established church. While the first five years of remissioning were some of my most difficult years of pastoral work, the following years of breakthrough have been some of the most awe-inspiring, humbling, and encouraging years of ministry I've ever experienced. Honestly, I didn't think pastoring could be filled with so much joy. The biggest change is what God has done in me to help me mature as a leader. I've learned to manage my own leadership anxiety with purpose, see through change processes that last years instead of trying to rush them, and seek support systems (spiritual directors, therapists, and intentional friendships) that help me to mature in who I am, how I lead, and how I resist the temptation to be at the center of the church instead of Christ.

The road of remissioning is not easy but it is good. I leave you with this prayer of Paul for the church in Ephesus, which was struggling to learn how to let go of its religious baggage and grow into maturity as the body of Christ. To my fellow remissioners: May you know that God's hope and power are capable of more than we could ever imagine. May God's goodness and humble power give you strength for the journey ahead:

> For this reason I kneel before the Father, from whom every family in heaven and on earth derives its name. I pray that out of his glorious riches he may strengthen you with power through his Spirit in your inner being, so that Christ may dwell in your hearts through faith. And I pray that you, being

rooted and established in love, may have power, together with all the Lord's holy people, to grasp how wide and long and high and deep is the love of Christ, and to know this love that surpasses knowledge—that you may be filled to the measure of all the fullness of God.

Now to him who is able to do immeasurably more than all we ask or imagine, according to his power that is at work within us, to him be glory in the church and in Christ Jesus throughout all generations, for ever and ever! Amen. (Eph 3:14-21)

ACKNOWLEDGMENTS

IN MY FIRST TWENTY YEARS OF MINISTRY, I'm fortunate to have served at two amazing churches. Cornerstone Baptist Church in Warrenton, Virginia, made room for me to learn, grow, and serve across many leadership positions. I had room to struggle, fail, innovate, and try again. Pastor Mike Poff, Andrea Jaffrey, and the leaders at Cornerstone helped me to believe that churches really could love people and a community with kindness. It was an honor to serve with you and thanks for sending me out with such generosity to my next assignment.

First Baptist Church Ashland has helped me understand the incredible power found in the death and resurrection of Jesus. When people ask me if miracles still happen, I tell them the story of our church and how God has worked through you for the sake of our neighbors. I have more hope in the resurrection power of Jesus because of you. There have been too many leaders over the past ten years to name, but I wouldn't be half of the person I am today without your courage, resilience, and hope. I didn't know that pastoring could be this joy-filled. It is a humbling gift to walk with you.

To the staff team at FBCA over these past ten years, you have been a remarkable gift to learn from, serve with, and lead. Rachel, you helped provide a soundtrack to remissioning and led with a giant heart. Laura, you helped us hold on to what was good and walk courageously into the future; thanks also for loving my two boys. Jimmie, you came in when things were tough and were a solid source of strength that helped us weather difficult challenges. Joanie, thanks for being eyes and ears as I was learning the work and for treating me like family. Daniel, you helped us rediscover joy and gave us language for how we can love our neighbors well. Jeremiah, you modeled how to serve well in crisis and love people even when it wasn't easy. Greg, thanks for sticking through all the changes and showing us how pipe organs can play in worship bands! Elena, who knew that starting as our accompanist could lead to running a nonprofit together and collaborating at the intersection of arts and church? Todd, you have modeled how to love people with generosity and be a kind friend. Bethany, thank you for leading with courage and for loving my children well. Ross, thanks for being such a joy to serve with—truly, it is such a gift to work with you, talk about music, and laugh. Lisa, your leadership roles have changed dramatically over the years and you've risen to the occasion every time; thank you for being so faithful to the work and becoming an example in our church for how to love our neighbors well. Tom, they say you shouldn't work with your friends—maybe people just need to make better friends. Thank you for being one of the most faithful, hopeful, and generous people I know. It is a privilege to work and coach soccer with you.

To Randell, getting to pastor in Ashland with you has been one of the most generous gifts from God in my life. Thank you for taking such courageous steps to partner, collaborate, and walk through so many ups and downs with me and FBCA. Thank you for leading Shiloh with such a big heart and making so much room for us all at the table. And perhaps most of all: thanks for being my friend.

To the team at V3, thanks for giving me the opportunity to build remissioning cohorts all those years ago. It was great to try and find the synergy between church planting, *The Church as Movement*, and remissioning. Thanks for giving me room to grow as a communicator, writer, and leader.

To Uptick, FXUS, and BGAV it has been a joy to learn with you and from you over the years. Thank you for helping invest in the lives of young leaders, spark kingdom initiatives, and make space for me to learn, lead, and grow.

To Brody Bond, the mo(µ)rning that made your music and this book possible over the years found its voice in our phone calls, texts, and friendship. Thank you for being a source of grace in my life all these years.

To Kathy, Gary, and Emily, I've known more of my life with you than without you. I have learned much about courage, strength, doing the right thing, and love by marrying into the family with you. Thank you for being so generous to me all these years.

To my mom and dad and my brothers, we've navigated a lot of storms over the years. Many of these pages are born out of what I learned growing up with you and facing the complexities of church life. Thank you for giving me room to grow.

To all my remissioning coaches over the years, Christy, Sterling, Mike, Cory, Matthew, Darryl, Trishonda, Austin, Dale, Taeler, Ray, Amy, and Ben: getting to serve with you, learn from you, coach these principles, and invest in church leaders from multiple countries together has taught me much about how diverse, good, and generous Jesus is and how much hope we can have as citizens of the kingdom of God. Kyuboem Lee, getting to write Remissioning 201 with you this year and serve alongside you has been both crazy (How did I think I could write this book and another curriculum at the same time?) and a centering practice that kept me rooted in friendship. Thank you, Kyuboem, for creating with me and being a bright light of the kingdom.

To my business partner, fellow author, and incredible friend, Eun Strawser, thank you for being a pastor and friend who helps me see the big picture and live faithfully on the ground. Here's to fostering kingdom collaborations and growing interdependence for years to come.

To Al Hsu, your wisdom, insight, and joy in helping this book come to life was a gift throughout the writing process. Thanks for making the editing process a great example of pruning for new life.

To Eli and Rowan, I experience so much joy in the world because of you. Each of you helps me see God through the way you treat people, serve generously, and seek the good in others. Here's to making more playlists, facing challenges, and choosing to love even when things aren't easy. I'm so grateful to be your dad. I love you.

To Shéy, I'm not sure how many disruptions to life we can face together, but none of the struggle is wasted when I get to walk through life with you. Thank you for helping me hear the still small voice of the Spirit, grow more resilient, and become a better person because of who you are. I see the beautiful kingdom moments of life because of how you live, love, and treat people. I'm so grateful to be your partner and to follow Jesus with you. I love you.

Lastly, big thanks to these musicians for providing a soundtrack throughout the writing process of this book: Brody Bond, Kendrick Lamar, Gillian Welch, Mavis Staples, Pedro the Lion, Rapsody, Sufjan Stevens, Mozart, Jason Isbell, Elmiene, The Wayward Leaves, Black Thought, Marcus Mumford, Kingfshr, Boy Genius, and The Brilliance.

NOTES

1. THE GIFT OF REMISSIONING

[1]Scott Neuman, "The Faithful See Both Crisis and Opportunity as Churches Close Across the Country," NPR, May 17, 2023, www.npr.org/2023/05/17/1175452002/church -closings-religious-affiliation.

[2]Edwin Friedman, *A Failure of Nerve: Leadership in the Age of the Quick Fix* (New York: Seabury Books, 2007), 32.

[3]Scott Thumma, "Twenty Years of Congregational Change: The 2020 Faith Communities Today Overview," Hartford Institute for Religion Research, 2020, https://faithcommu nitiestoday.org/wp-content/uploads/2021/10/Faith-Communities-Today-2020 -Summary-Report.pdf; Aaron Earls, "Protestant Church Closures Outpace Opening in U.S.," Lifeway Research, May 25, 2021, https://research.lifeway.com/2021/05/25 /protestant-church-closures-outpace-openings-in-u-s; Aaron Earls, "Pastors and Churches Face Historic Lack of Trust," Lifeway Research, July 12, 2022, https://research .lifeway.com/2022/07/12/pastors-and-churches-face-historic-lack-of-trust.

2. REMISSIONING THROUGH DESCENT

[1]Simon Sinek, *Leaders Eat Last* (Chicago: Portfolio Penguin, 2017).

[2]Henri Nouwen, *In the Name of Jesus: Reflections on Christian Leadership* (New York: Crossroad Company, 1989), 77.

[3]Nouwen, *In the Name of Jesus*, 43-44.

[4]Brené Brown, *Atlas of the Heart* (New York: Random House, 2021), 137.

3. FINDING OURSELVES IN THE REMISSIONING STORY

[1]Henri Nouwen, *Reaching Out: The Three Movements of the Spiritual Life* (New York: Doubleday, 1975), 52.

4. REMISSIONERS SHIFT FROM OWNERSHIP TO STEWARDSHIP

[1]Thank you to Mike Poff for this wisdom!

[2]Peter Scazzero, *The Emotionally Healthy Church: A Strategy for Discipleship that Actually Changes Lives* (Grand Rapids, MI: Zondervan, 2010), 206-7.

[3]Scazzero, *Emotionally Healthy Church*, 205.

[4]Gordon MacDonald, *Who Stole My Church?: What to Do When the Church You Love Tries to Enter the 21st Century* (Nashville: Thomas Nelson, 2011).

[5]JR Woodward and Dan White Jr., *The Church as Movement: Starting and Sustaining Missional-Incarnational Communities* (Downers Grove, IL: InterVarsity Press, 2016), 79.

[6]David Fitch, *Seven Practices for the Church on Mission* (Downers Grove, IL: InterVarsity Press, 2018), 53.

5. CREATIVE DESTRUCTION: REMISSIONING FROM DEATH TO LIFE

[1]Joseph A. Schumpeter, *Capitalism, Socialism, and Democracy*, 3rd ed. (New York: Harper Perennial Modern Classics, 2008 [1942]).

[2]Chunka Mui, "How Kodak Failed," Forbes, January 18, 2012, www.forbes.com/sites/chunkamui/2012/01/18/how-kodak-failed.

[3]Joshua Hayden, *Creative Destruction: Towards a Theology of Institutions* (DMin diss., Duke University, 2016), 6, http://hdl.handle.net/10161/12918.

[4]NASA, "July 20, 1969: One Giant Leap for Mankind," last updated June 13, 2024, www.nasa.gov/mission_pages/apollo/apollo11.html.

[5]Sustainable Human, "How Wolves Change Rivers," February 13, 2014, YouTube video, 4:33, www.youtube.com/watch?v=ysa5OBhXz-Q.

[6]Hayden, *Creative Destruction*, 57-58.

[7]Erica Berry, "What Can Americans Agree On? Wolves," *New York Times*, January 30, 2024, www.nytimes.com/2024/01/30/opinion/wolves-repopulation-colorado-polarization.html.

[8]Michael Jinkins, *The Church Faces Death: Ecclesiology in a Post-Modern Context* (New York: Oxford University Press, 2004), 30.

[9]"Adoption Merger—A Vote Has Been Called," Mill City Church, November 23, 2022, https://millcitychurch.com/adoption-merger-a-vote-has-been-called.

[10]Old Town Community Church, "Annual Report 2024," February 11, 2024, https://oldtown.cc/wp-content/uploads/2024/02/2024-Annual-Report_Feb2024.pdf.

6. REMISSIONING WITH FRESH EYES

[1]Dallas Willard, *The Divine Conspiracy: Rediscovering Our Hidden Life in God* (San Francisco: HarperSanFrancisco, 1997), 58.

7. PRUNING FOR GROWTH IN THE REMISSIONING GARDEN

[1]This section is adapted from Joshua Hayden, *Creative Destruction: Towards a Theology of Institutions* (DMin diss., Duke University, 2016), 97-125, http://hdl.handle.net/10161/12918.

[2]Andy Crouch, *Playing God: Redeeming the Gift of Power* (Downers Grove, IL: InterVarsity Press, 2013), 199.

[3]Crouch, *Playing God*, 200.

[4]Seth Godin, "Life, the Internet, and Everything," *On Being*, hosted by Krista Tippett, podcast, January 24, 2013, https://onbeing.org/programs/seth-godin-life-the-internet-and-everything-sep2018.

8. The Nature of Change in the Remissioning Journey

[1]Eun Strawser, *Centering Discipleship: A Pathway for Multiplying Spectators into Mature Disciples* (Downers Grove, IL: InterVarsity Press, 2023), 40.

[2]See Strawser, 40-43, for further discussion of discipleship pathways and how these leadership markers affect community.

[3]Barna, "Almost Half of Practicing Christian Millennials Say Evangelism Is Wrong," February 5, 2019, www.barna.com/research/millennials-oppose-evangelism.

[4]Hugh Heclo, *On Thinking Institutionally* (New York: Oxford University Press, 2008), 11-43.

[5]Heclo, *On Thinking Institutionally*, 7.

[6]Heclo, *On Thinking Institutionally*, 25.

[7]Ronald A. Heifetz and Marty Linsky, *Leadership on the Line: Staying Alive Through the Dangers of Leading* (Cambridge, MA: Harvard Business School Press, 2002), https://hbswk.hbs.edu/archive/leadership-on-the-line-staying-alive-through-the-dangers -of-leading.

[8]Edwin Friedman, *A Failure of Nerve: Leadership in the Age of the Quick Fix* (New York: Seabury Books, 2007), 27.

[9]Friedman, *A Failure of Nerve*, 188.

9. Remissioning Starts with the End

[1]L. Gregory Jones, "Traditioned Innovation," Faith & Leadership, Duke Divinity School, January 19, 2009, https://faithandleadership.com/traditioned-innovation-0.

[2]This section is adapted from Joshua Hayden, *Creative Destruction: Towards a Theology of Institutions* (DMin diss., Duke University, 2016), 9-24, http://hdl.handle.net/10161 /12918.

[3]There is an argument to be made that learning the prayer through listening to the congregation is itself part of the practice of learning the institutional language. Yet in our cultural context, fewer and fewer people are willing to take the time to learn the church's language without it being more easily accessible.

[4]James K. A. Smith, *Desiring the Kingdom: Worship, Worldview, and Cultural Formation* (Grand Rapids, MI: Baker Academic, 2009), 83.

[5]Smith, *Desiring the Kingdom*, 89.

[6]Hayden, *Creative Destruction*, 75-76.

10. Remissioning and the Work of Remembering

[1]Southern Poverty Law Center, "Whose Heritage? Public Symbols of the Confederacy," February 1, 2019, www.splcenter.org/20190201/whose-heritage-public-symbols -confederacy.

[2]Beth Ann Gaede, *Ending with Hope: A Resource for Closing Congregations* (Bethesda, MD: Alban Institute, 2002), 10.

[3]Saint Benedict, *The Rule of Saint Benedict*, ed. Leonard J. Doyle (Collegeville, MN: Order of Saint Benedict, 1948), IV.47. This section is adapted from Joshua Hayden, *Creative Destruction: Towards a Theology of Institutions* (DMin diss., Duke University, 2016), 77-79, http://hdl.handle.net/10161/12918.

[4]L. Gregory Jones, "Traditioned Innovation," Faith & Leadership, Duke Divinity School, January 19, 2009, https://faithandleadership.com/traditioned-innovation-0.

[5]L. Gregory Jones and Nathan Jones, "Deep Trends Affecting Christian Institutions," Faith & Leadership, Duke Divinity School, https://www.faithandleadership.com /l-gregory-jones-and-nathan-jones-deep-trends-affecting-christian-institutions.

[6]Michael Jinkins, *The Church Faces Death: Ecclesiology in a Post-Modern Context* (New York: Oxford University Press, 1999), 20.

[7]This section is adapted from Hayden, *Creative Destruction*, 81-85.

[8]Jones, "Traditioned Innovation."

[9]L. Gregory Jones, "Why Institutions Matter," Faith & Leadership, Duke Divinity School, March 1, 2009, www.faithandleadership.com/content/why-institutions-matter.

[10]L. Gregory Jones and Célestin Musekura, *Forgiving as We've Been Forgiven: Community Practices for Making Peace* (Downers Grove, IL: InterVarsity Press, 2010), 94.

[11]Jones and Musekura, *Forgiving as We've Been Forgiven*, 87.

[12]Jacqueline Novogratz, *The Blue Sweater: Bridging the Gap between Rich and Poor in an Interconnected World* (Emmaus, PA: Rodale, 2009), 217.

[13]Novogratz, *Blue Sweater*, 164.

11. BURYING PREFERENCES FOR THE SAKE OF MISSION

[1]Bob Dylan, "Gotta Change My Way of Thinking," *Slow Train Coming*, Columbia, 1979.

[2]This section is adapted from Joshua Hayden, *Creative Destruction: Towards a Theology of Institutions* (DMin diss., Duke University, 2016), 97-125, http://hdl.handle.net/10161 /12918.

[3]Seth Godin, "The Race to the Bottom," Seth's Blog, August 20, 2012, https://seths .blog/2012/08/the-race-to-the-bottom.

[4]Marva J. Dawn, *The Sense of the Call: A Sabbath Way of Life for Those Who Serve God, the Church, and the World* (Grand Rapids, MI: Eerdmans, 2006), 35.

[5]Jad Abumrad, Robert Krulwich, and Suzanne Simard, "From Tree to Shining Tree," *Radiolab*, podcast transcript, July 30, 2016, https://radiolab.org/podcast/from-tree-to -shining-tree/transcript.

[6]Abumrad, Krulwich, and Simard, "From Tree to Shining Tree."

[7]Martin Luther King Jr., "Letter from Birmingham Jail," in *A Testament of Hope: The Essential Writings and Speeches of Martin Luther King Jr.*, ed. James M. Washington (New York: HarperCollins, 1991), 290. King says, "Injustice anywhere is a threat to justice everywhere. We are caught in an inescapable network of mutuality, tied in a single garment of destiny. Whatever affects one directly affects all indirectly."

12. Everything Is Liturgical (So Remission on Purpose!)

[1]This section is adapted from Joshua Hayden, *Creative Destruction: Towards a Theology of Institutions* (DMin diss., Duke University, 2016), 9-25, http://hdl.handle.net/10161/12918.

[2]James K. A. Smith, *Desiring the Kingdom: Worship, Worldview, and Cultural Formation*, Volume 1 of Cultural Liturgies (Grand Rapids, MI: Baker Academic, 2009), 17-18.

[3]Smith, *Desiring the Kingdom*, 52.

[4]Smith, *Desiring the Kingdom*, 56.

13. The Four Spaces of Belonging in a Remissioning Context

[1]Robin Dunbar, "Dunbar's Number," *New Scientist*, accessed June 12, 2024, www.newscientist.com/definition/dunbars-number.

[2]Carey Nieuwhof, "The Top 8 Reasons Most Churches Never Break the 200 Attendance Mark," Carey Nieuwhof (blog), copyright 2024, https://careynieuwhof.com/the-8-most-common-reasons-most-churches-never-break-the-200-attendance-mark.

[3]Joseph R. Myers, *The Search to Belong: Rethinking Intimacy, Community, and Small Groups* (Grand Rapids, MI: Zondervan, 2003), 38.

[4]Myers, *Search to Belong*, 39.

[5]Eun Kyong Strawser, *Centering Discipleship: A Pathway for Multiplying Spectators into Mature Disciples* (Downers Grove, IL: InterVarsity Press, 2023), 143-68; Dan White Jr. and JR Woodward, *The Church as Movement: Starting and Sustaining Missional-Incarnational Communities* (Downers Grove, IL: InterVarsity Press, 2016), 156.

[6]Hartford Institute for Religion Research, "Fast Facts about American Religion," http://hirr.hartsem.edu/research/fastfacts/fast_facts.html, accessed June 15, 2024.

14. Creating Shared Experiments to Grow
a Remissioning Imagination

[1]Makoto Fujimura, *Culture Care* (Salem, MA: Fujimura Institute and International Arts Movement, 2014), 81. This section is adapted from Joshua Hayden, *Creative Destruction: Towards a Theology of Institutions* (DMin diss., Duke University, 2016), 97-125, http://hdl.handle.net/10161/12918.

[2]Fujimura, *Culture Care*, 82.

[3]Fujimura, *Culture Care*, 83.

[4]Charles Duhigg, *The Power of Habit: Why We Do What We Do in Life and Business* (New York: Random House, 2012), 244.

[5]Peter F. Drucker, *Managing the Nonprofit Organization: Practices and Principles* (New York: HarperCollins, 1990), 11.

[6]Matthew E. May, "The Rules of Successful Skunk Works Projects," *Fast Company*, October 9, 2012, www.fastcompany.com/3001702/rules-successful-skunk-works-projects.

15. Movemental Discipleship for Remissioning Churches

[1]Alan Deutschman, *Change or Die: The Three Keys to Change at Work and in Life* (New York: Regan, 2007).

16. Race, Class, and the Kingdom of God Are Essential for Remissioning

[1]Willie James Jennings, *Acts* (Louisville, KY: Westminster John Knox Press, 2017), 6.
[2]Latasha Morrison, *Be The Bridge: Pursuing God's Heart for Racial Reconciliation* (Colorado Springs, CO: Waterbrook, 2019), 2-3.
[3]Benjamin Campbell, *Richmond's Unhealed History* (Richmond, VA: Brandylane Publishers, 2012).
[4]James Cone, *Black Theology & Black Power* (Maryknoll, NY: Orbis, 2006), 81.
[5]Martin Luther King Jr., *A Testament of Hope: The Essential Writings and Speeches of Martin Luther King Jr.*, ed. James M. Washington (New York: HarperCollins, 1991), 263.
[6]Ken Wytsma, *The Myth of Equality: Uncovering the Roots of Injustice and Privilege* (Downers Grove, IL: InterVarsity Press, 2017), 94-95.

17. Habits + Vision = Remissioning

[1]Why don't denomination and association leaders have the same call to remission established churches as we do to start new churches? Why don't we commit to the long, steady work of transforming existing churches so we might see systems change and not just individuals and individual churches? Where are the leaders willing to sow seeds for remissioning trees whose shade they may not enjoy?
[2]Tod Bolsinger, *Canoeing the Mountains: Christian Leadership in Uncharted Territory* (Downers Grove, IL: InterVarsity Press, 2015), 40-41.
[3]Ronald Heifetz and Marty Linsky, *Leadership on the Line: Staying Alive Through the Dangers of Change* (Boston: Harvard Business School Press, 2017), 20.
[4]Heifetz and Linsky, *Leadership on the Line*, 27.

18. Embracing Conflict as Remissioning Leaders

[1]Lew Feldman, "I'm Glad You Asked: Reaction Wood," University of California Botanical Garden at Berkeley, March 1, 2020, https://botanicalgarden.berkeley.edu/glad-you -asked/reaction-wood.
[2]Carl Zimmer, "The Lost History of One of the World's Strangest Science Experiments," *New York Times*, March 29, 2019, www.nytimes.com/2019/03/29/sunday-review /biosphere-2-climate-change.html.
[3]Mark Nelson, *Pushing Our Limits: Insights from Biosphere 2* (Tucson: University of Arizona Press, 2018), 128.
[4]Tod Bolsinger, *Canoeing the Mountains: Christian Leadership in Uncharted Territory* (Downers Grove, IL: Intervarsity Press, 2015), 136-37.

[5]James P. Osterhaus, Joseph M. Jurkowski, and Todd A. Hahn, *Thriving Through Ministry Conflict: A Parable on How Resistance Can Be Your Ally* (Grand Rapids, MI: Zondervan, 2005), 14.

[6]Edwin Friedman, *A Failure of Nerve: Leadership in the Age of the Quick Fix* (New York: Seabury Books, 2007), 32.

[7]Bolsinger, *Canoeing the Mountains*, 135-49.

[8]Edwin Friedman, *Failure of Nerve*, 163.

[9]Fred Luskin, *Forgive for Good: A Proven Prescription for Health and Happiness* (New York: HarperSanFrancisco, 2002), 39.

19. An Open Invitation for Remissioning Leaders

[1]Susan Bigelow Reynolds, "Everybody Wants a Revolution, but Nobody Wants to Do the Dishes," *The Atlantic*, May 23, 2019, www.theatlantic.com/ideas/archive/2019/05 /carroll-was-wrong-about-change-catholic-church/590080.

[2]James P. Osterhaus, Joseph M. Jurkowski, and Todd A. Hahn, *Thriving Through Ministry Conflict: A Parable on How Resistance Can Be Your Ally* (Grand Rapids, MI: Zondervan, 2005), 63.

[3]Brené Brown, *Braving the Wilderness: The Quest for True Belonging and the Courage to Stand Alone* (New York: Random House, 2017), 154.

20. A Remissioning Path Requires New Metrics

[1]Gil Rendle, *Doing the Math of Mission: Fruits, Faithfulness, and Metrics* (Lanham, MD: Rowman & Littlefield, 2014), 14.

[2]Rendle, *Doing the Math of Mission*, 16.

21. Four Pathways for Remissioning

[1]This section is adapted from Joshua Hayden, *Creative Destruction: Towards a Theology of Institutions* (DMin diss., Duke University, 2016), 97-125, http://hdl.handle.net/10161 /12918.

[2]Flatlands Reformed Church, "Our History," accessed June 22, 2024, www.flatlands reformed.org/our-history.

[3]L. Gregory Jones, "Overcome Mission Drift by Practicing Traditioned Innovation," Faith & Leadership, Duke Divinity School, November 17, 2015, www.faithandleadership .com/l-gregory-jones-overcome-mission-drift-practicing-traditioned-innovation.

[4]St. Luke's Church, "The Story of St. Luke's," copyright 2023, www.stlukese16.co.uk /history.

[5]Greg Jones and C. Kavin Rowe, *Thriving Communities: The Pattern of Church Life Then and Now* (Durham, NC: Faith & Leadership, 2014), loc. 66-68, Kindle.

[6]Convergence, "History," copyright 2013, https://ourconvergence.org/about/history.

[7]Convergence, "History."

[8]Convergence, "History."

[9]Find out more at St. John Center for Homeless Men, www.stjohncenter.org/about-us/.

[10]St. John Center for Homeless Men.

22. Dying to Live

[1]Christ City Church, "Serve the Community," accessed June 24, 2024, www.christcitydc .org/serve-the-community.

ABOUT THE AUTHOR

Rev. Dr. Joshua Hayden is the lead pastor of First Baptist Church Ashland and copresident of 'Iwa Collaborative. Josh has over twenty years' experience in organizational leadership and has worked and led in nonprofit, church plant, and established church settings. Josh studied leadership and organizational change while writing *Creative Destruction: Towards a Theology of Institutions* to receive a doctorate from Duke Divinity School. He is also the author of *Sacred Hope*, a book designed to foster conversation around the role of hope in our everyday lives. Josh is a sought-out voice of leadership in the church, ecumenically wide denominations, seminaries, national network boards, and local community boards. He is married to his best friend and high school sweetheart, Shéy, and they have two sons, Rowan and Eli, who are the best part of their every day.

Josh has been the director and developer of Remissioning Collectives, a thirty-week learning experience that brings five to eight established church pastors, seminary students, church planters, and intentional interim leaders to journey together on the courageous and innovative work of remissioning churches. In addition, he has developed countless tools, policies, and protocols that systematically and practically help church leadership navigate change well.

Socials:

Instagram @joshua_r_hayden

Facebook @joshuahaydenauthor

josh@fbcava.org

josh@iwacollaborative.com

@iwacollaborative

remissioningchurches.com

Missio Alliance

Missio Alliance has arisen in response to the shared voice of pastors and ministry leaders from across the landscape of North American Christianity for a new "space" of togetherness and reflection amid the issues and challenges facing the church in our day. We are united by a desire for a fresh expression of evangelical faith, one significantly informed by the global evangelical family. Lausanne's Cape Town Commitment, "A Confession of Faith and a Call to Action," provides an excellent guidepost for our ethos and aims.

Through partnerships with schools, denominational bodies, ministry organizations, and networks of churches and leaders, Missio Alliance addresses the most vital theological and cultural issues facing the North American church in God's mission today. We do this primarily by convening gatherings, curating resources, and catalyzing innovation in leadership formation.

Rooted in the core convictions of evangelical orthodoxy, the ministry of Missio Alliance is animated by a strong and distinctive theological identity that emphasizes

Comprehensive Mutuality: Advancing the partnered voice and leadership of women and men among the beautiful diversity of the body of Christ across the lines of race, culture, and theological heritage.

Hopeful Witness: Advancing a way of being the people of God in the world that reflects an unwavering and joyful hope in the lordship of Christ in the church and over all things.

Church in Mission: Advancing a vision of the local church in which our identity and the power of our testimony is found and expressed through our active participation in God's mission in the world.

In partnership with InterVarsity Press, we are pleased to offer a line of resources authored by a diverse range of theological practitioners. The resources in this series are selected based on the important way in which they address and embody these values, and thus, the unique contribution they offer in equipping Christian leaders for fuller and more faithful participation in God's mission.

missioalliance.org | twitter.com/missioalliance | facebook.com/missioalliance

More Titles from
InterVarsity Press and Missio Alliance

**Finding Freedom
in Constraint**
978-1-5140-0431-9

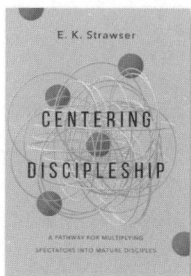

**Centering
Discipleship**
978-1-5140-0706-8

**Faithful
Politics**
978-1-5140-0749-5

Together in Ministry
978-1-5140-0070-0

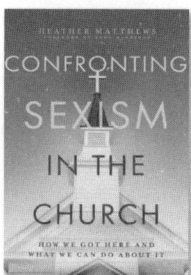

**Confronting Sexism
in the Church**
978-1-5140-0818-8

Plundered
978-1-5140-0774-7

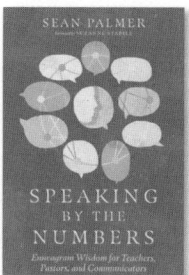

**Speaking by
the Numbers**
978-0-8308-4166-0

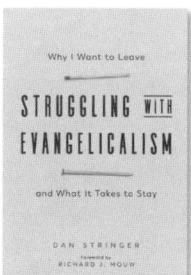

**Struggling with
Evangelicalism**
978-0-8308-4766-2